Arleen Westerhof has written a [...]
will open the doors to revelation [...]
Christians. *Impact* is simply brilli[...]

    – *Dr. Cindy Jacobs*
      Generals International

For years the gifts of the Holy Spirit have been poured out upon the Body of Christ, enabling us to do the works of Jesus Christ. But too often our containers are too small, our wineskins are old, and our mindsets are limited. Now, along come a new generation of forerunners, preparing the way for clear revelation with fresh applications. That is exactly what you will find in this book. Thank you Arleen for providing a contemporary example of how we can work revelation into a transformational model. Well done!

    – *Dr. James W. Goll*
      Founder of God Encounters Ministries and GOLL Ideation LLC,
      international author, recording artist, and communications trainer

The prophets of our time are courageous, strong and intentional in their faithful proclamation of the word of the Lord. They do this in the midst of the chaos and confusion in our governments and societies. As they listen to the Father's voice and obey His instructions, they are changing the direction of nations and seeing God's Kingdom manifested in new ways. Arleen Westerhof is such a prophet. She not only clearly hears the Father's voice, but boldly acts on His commands. And she does this with a Spirit-filled grace that brings life.

I encourage you to read this book with an expectant heart. Ask God to give you a vision that will require a supernatural move of the Spirit to achieve it, then watch God work together with you to accomplish great things. I believe that this is our Kingdom watershed moment in history. The army of God in the marketplace and the church has the ability to see God's Kingdom come to earth.

    – *Dr. Graham Power*
      Founder of Global Day of Prayer and Unashamedly Ethical
      Executive Chair of Power Group of Companies

One of the fascinating developments of our times is the increasing focus on prophecy and the creation of prophetic cultures. In *Impact* Arleen Westerhof describes her personal journey in this area. As you read, you will soon be gripped by the testimonies of God speaking.

But it goes further than the local church! If Christ is King over every area of life and society, then He also speaks about all of these areas. It is remarkable how God's Spirit is calling modern-day Daniels who are positioned in the middle of both the church and society. They speak out revelation from God's throne, often with surprising results. A fascinating book that will strengthen your faith! Highly recommended.

— *Machiel Jonker*
Chairman, Assemblies of God, the Netherlands

Arleen Westerhof has always been a great communicator, but *Impact* is more than communicating a message – it's about a new move of God on the earth. As Arleen says, it's not just enough to think big anymore – we have to think differently. This book is full of practical insights into this new move of God and the role of prophecy in it. Nothing short of destiny mobilization for influencing your world is found within the pages of this book. You will want to share it with others and you will refer to it often.

— *Dr. Sharon Stone*
Presiding Apostle, Christian International Europe

I highly recommend *Impact*. Arleen Westerhof writes about prophecy in a way that is accessible for everyone, but that also shows that it is a serious matter that you must deal with responsibly. God's people are supposed to be prophetic, and through prophecy our generation has the chance to reveal God's heart in both the church and in society. Prophecy helps us to make the earth look a little bit more like heaven. As you learn to understand His voice and obey Him, God's Kingdom breaks through in your own life and in the world around you. A new perspective!

— *Gerlo Sogtoen*
Chairman, Pastoral Core Group,
Catholic Charismatic Renewal, the Netherlands

"Compelling" is the word that best describes *Impact*. When you start reading this book you won't want to put it down. It is compelling because of its honesty, humility, integrity, and truth. Arleen Westerhof has spent many years helping others understand and walk in the revelation that comes from the voice of God. You will find personal stories of twenty-first-century global leaders who have been positioned by God because of their practical application of prophetic revelation. *Impact* will demystify something that Jesus tells us is one of our rights of citizenship in the Kingdom: "My sheep hear My voice, and I know them, and they follow Me ..." There are hidden treasures waiting for you as you read this book!

– *Paul L. Cuny*
President MarketPlace Leadership International
Author of "Secrets of the Kingdom Economy" and "Nehemiah People"

Dr. Arleen Westerhof has written an important book for our times. Over the years, I have watched Arleen build movements, change personal destinies, and influence world leaders by working with the revelation God has given her. This book will equip you to impact your world in ways you never dreamed possible. Thoroughly biblical, it gives foundations to change the world you live in.

– *Stacey Campbell*
Founder Canadian Prophetic Council

Impact empowers prophets and prophetic believers to present God's answers and solutions in these times of great change and social upheaval. These answers are not for the Church alone. Thinking from a Kingdom perspective, Arleen connects God's words with the future of the economy, government, media, culture, and even whole cities and nations.

Read this book and gain a better understanding of the crucial role of prophecy and prophets in the body of Christ and the world we live in. Let a deep desire grow within you for true reformation and change, brought about by the miraculous guidance of the Holy Spirit. And most of all, take to heart the call to action: "earnestly desire the spiritual gifts, especially that you may prophesy" (1 Cor. 14:1).

– *Hans Maat*
Director, Evangelisch Werkverband binnen
de Protestantse Kerk in Nederland

Arleen Westerhof is a prophetic pioneer whose keen sense of the times and seasons and ability to communicate the heart of God have allowed her to impact thousands. Arleen is a dear friend and trusted prophetic voice in my life and ministry. Her accuracy in the prophetic comes from a place of deep intimacy with the Holy Spirit.

I believe that *Impact* will challenge and change your life, business, family and ministry. This is a very significant book for the church in our time.

> – *David Wagner*
> Father's Heart Ministries

This book is very timely and important! The time has come for us to call forth the prophets. Read this book and understand the difference between hearing God's voice and acting in the gift of prophecy. Whether you are a prophet or a prophetic Christian, allow God to lead you into a fuller understanding of His calling for you in this hour.

Let us read, discuss and seek the Lord together across the five-fold ministry. In today's battlefield, the marketplace, we can humbly serve God together, grateful for all his gifts.

> – *Jan Sturesson*
> International strategy consultant
> Chairman of the International Board, Christian Chamber
> of Commerce International

Arleen Westerhof came from a traditional Christian background before discovering the power of the Holy Spirit. His presence, the supernatural and the prophetic are now part of her daily life. Her scientific background helps her to give a clear and sound representation of the work and the Person of the Holy Spirit and of prophecy in particular.

Impact is an absolute must for everyone who wants more from God and who wonders about the importance of prophecy. A few of the topics covered in this book are: the apostolic/prophetic foundations, protocol and prophecy in the local church and in the place where God has placed you, and the importance of character in ministry. A fascinating and important book and an asset to our country.

> – *Hans Tims*
> National Leader of Friends for Ministries in Fellowship, the Netherlands

IMPACT

ARLEEN WESTERHOF

ARROWZ

impact verb

im·pact | \ im-'pakt \

impacted; impacting; impacts

Definition of *impact* (Entry 1 of 2)

transitive verb

1   a   : to fix firmly by or as if by packing or wedging
      b   : to press together
2   a   : to have a direct effect or impact on : impinge on
      b   : to strike forcefully
          also : to cause to strike forcefully

intransitive verb

1   : to have an impact —often used with on
2   : to impinge or make contact especially forcefully

impact noun

im·pact | \ 'im-'pakt \

Definition of *impact* (Entry 2 of 2)

1   a   : an impinging or striking especially of one body
          against another
      b   : a forceful contact or onset
          also : the impetus communicated in or as if in such
              a contact
2   : the force of impression of one thing on another:
          a significant or major effect
          // the *impact* of science on our society
          // an environmental *impact* study

Impact
– Prophesy and Change the World

Copyright © 2019 Arleen Westerhof

Published by Arrowz USA in conjunction with Mandate Publishing, Amsterdam
info@arrowz.org
www.arrowz.org

Author: Arleen Westerhof
Art direction and interior design: Ronald Gabrielsen, 3ig.com

ISBN 978 1 951014 01 8

Printed in the United States of America

Contents

Foreword

We are living in exciting and terrifying times: the genuine children of God are being revealed. The Holy Spirit speaks and divinely inspires us. This allows us to inform, impart and impact the world around us. It is important that every believer hears the voice of God. This is the foundation of the prophetic. From this groundwork, prophecy interacts with the world around us to generate Kingdom legacy. Through this we are able to permeate every aspect of life and every sphere of culture. Prophecy gives birth to life-giving declarations and effective and innovative strategies.

The prophet Elijah encountered the presence of God in a whisper. This still, small voice held the revelation and activation. It led to transformation in society. Through Jesus we have open access to the Holy Spirit. Now the spiritual gift of prophecy is available to all of us!

The impact prophecy has in my life is profound and personal, and I believe it can have the same degree of impact on yours. Throughout my walk with the Lord, major life decisions were catalyzed by notable prophetic words. God led me to my beautiful wife through a personal collection of prophetic words. An unforgettable divine encounter led us to take steps of faith that moved my family cross-country to southern California, because we believe God will bring revival and a great harvest there. Prophetic promises from this encounter still resonate: ministries I steward today were birthed from these prophetic seeds. By following His voice, the Lord has prospered and blessed me through every step of obedient faith. I can testify to this truth: God is not distant, but desires to be intimately involved in our lives.

From industry and business, family and education, to governments and ecosystems, the prophetic is key to unlocking

God's perspective. It activates divine connections for Kingdom transformation. God is raising up revivalists and reformers who are deeply in love with Jesus and in tune with the Holy Spirit.

My good friend and beloved sister-in-Christ, Arleen Westerhof, has put together this excellent and valuable resource. I believe this will give you the tools and inspiration to increase in prophetic proficiency. Arleen is a long-time prophetic voice in the apostolic arena of Harvest International Ministry. Her insight into the prophetic will give you a clear understanding of how prophecy can transform your everyday lives. She and her husband Dick impact their spheres of influence through their ministry God's Embassy Amsterdam. They have a call to bring societal transformation through personal prophetic ministry. From social issues to economic innovations that are impacting nations, their prophetic and apostolic anointings are transforming their region with the light of God's love.

As you read ahead, may the revelations and testimonies in this book enrich your personal journey of discovering the prophetic hand-in-hand with Abba Father. As with the sons of Issachar (see 1 Chron. 12:32), I believe God is raising you up as sons and daughters to understand the signs and times, so that you know what to do. I believe the principles presented here by Arleen provide the tools for practical application and personal reflection. These will encourage you to seek the voice of God and hear Him with clarity and purpose. This book is a timely word for this due season. I am excited that the Lord has led you to read this. May you step into your prophetic potential with faith for the fullness of God and His love through you.

In His love,

– *Dr. Ché Ahn*
Senior Pastor, HRock Church, Pasadena
President, Harvest International Ministry
International Chancellor, Wagner University

Working with Revelation

"This is the most beautiful thing I've ever heard," said the lady in the row behind me as she softly started to cry. A few moments later a man on the other side of the room stood up and said, "Hallelujah, this is unbelievable!" He put both hands over his mouth and sat down embarrassed at his own outburst. As the speaker continued, another woman stood up and ran out of the room. I heard her talking to someone on her mobile phone: "I'm so excited I can't sit still! This is amazing! You have to hear this!" She stuck her hand with the phone into the room. And so it went. I could have understood all this excitement if we had been in a revival meeting. But we weren't. We were in an economic summit and the Holy Spirit had just fallen.

The attendees were Christian professors and leaders in the fields of economics, government and business. They were not charismatic Christians. The lecture was about economic principles, but God's presence was tangible. God was revealing new ideas, moving the participants to their cores.

A few years earlier the Lord started to wake me up in the middle of the night. He said: "Call forth the Josephs and Daniels in business and economics! I want to heal nations by healing their economies."

I didn't understand. "Lord, why on earth do you want me to pray for Mammon?"[1] I said out loud. Back then I had no idea that God was so interested in business and economics. I still thought that they were the domain of Mammon and that I should stay as far away from them as possible. God, however, had other ideas. He continued to wake me up three or four times a week, every week, for two years!

Each time He woke me up I'd pray until the burden for prayer lifted and then I'd go back to bed. Finally, after two years He said, "And now, Arleen, I want *you* to ask me for the solutions to heal business and economics."

Did I hear that right? I blurted out, "Lord, I've got a Ph.D. in chemistry, not economics, remember?"

He raised His voice and said: "Ask!" It wasn't a suggestion.

These prophetic encounters became the foundation for what would later become the Economic Summit, an organization committed to seeing God heal nations by healing their economies and their societies. The new supernaturally inspired blueprints that God is releasing through the summits are attracting attention worldwide. Even secular governments are coming around to the fact that these are truly transformational blueprints for nations—and they tell us so!

Divine revelation has led us to start more than just the Economic Summit. People often ask my husband and me, "How do you do it? How are you able to consistently take the revelation that God gives you and make it practical in a way that changes people's lives, their cities and even their nations?" Early on I realized that the prophetic was one of the keys to changing nations. However, transforming society requires more than just being able to hear God's voice. We have to learn how to receive divine revelation and make it practical. In other words, we have to learn how to "work with revelation."

As I've learned to work with revelation I have seen God use me, my husband, and our church to see measurable change for good come in Amsterdam's Red Light District. Following His voice has helped us to start new ministries, new foundations and new businesses in the nations. It has also helped our church to become an apostolic center that is releasing people into their callings in every sphere of influence in society.

A New Situation

We are at a watershed moment in history. The tricky thing about watershed moments is that we often don't recognize that we're in them until they are over. This time around the watershed moment is being caused by the current techno-logical revolution. New technologies such as Artificial Intelligence, robotics, self-driving cars and the "Internet of Things" (IoT, which refers to the situation in which all sorts of physical devices and everyday objects are connected through the internet and are independently communicating with each other) are changing the way we live, work and communicate with each other beyond all recognition.

In a previous watershed moment, the Industrial Revolution, the rise of the steam engine (1768)[2] was responsible for new jobs being created in industries that had never existed before. Many of these jobs, however, were in the cities. Within fifty years Great Britain's population went from 70 percent of the population living in the country to 70 percent of the population living in the cities. The social disruption created by thousands upon thousands of people moving into the cities in search of work was evident, among other things, in the extreme poverty and the "poorhouses" that characterized that period.

Many are calling the era we now live in the "Fourth Industrial Revolution." This revolution has the potential to lead to more disruption than all of the other industrial revolutions of the past. This is because of:

1. The *speed* at which changes are occurring. The deeply interconnected world that we live in is causing the speed at which changes occur to exceed anything that we have ever seen before in the history of the planet.
2. The *breadth* and the *depth* of these changes. The digital revolution is causing unprecedented paradigm shifts in the economy, business, society and individual lives. It is not only changing "what" and "how" we do things, but "who" we think we are.
3. *Transformed systems.* This revolution is transforming entire systems (government, economics, business, education, etc.) within and across countries, companies, industries and society as a whole.[3]

What this boils down to is that about 47 percent of the jobs that now exist in the US (and in other nations) are at risk of being made obsolete by these new technologies in the next decade or two. Even though new jobs in new industries will be created, the expectation is that jobs in old industries will become obsolete at a much faster rate than that these new jobs will be created.[4] You don't have to be a rocket scientist to know that this means that there is trouble on the horizon.

In the midst of all this social upheaval God is pouring out His Spirit. He is igniting the prophetic in a whole new way all over the world and He wants us to know that heaven is not in crisis. Since He never does anything without first revealing it to His servants, the prophets (Amos 3:7), He wants to prepare us by giving us revelation and strategies for the future. That's why we are seeing the Holy Spirit opening up opportunities for the body of Christ to function in the prophetic in new ways. Prophets are starting to turn up as advisors in government, media, entertainment, think tanks and even business and economics. With these opportunities, however, come new challenges and new requirements for prophets.

Schools of the Prophets

Shortly after Dick and I started our church God's Embassy Amsterdam in 2005, I knew that I needed to train people in the prophetic so that they could step into these areas with confidence. At first I thought about using some of the existing prophetic courses that I knew about. Very quickly, however, I realized that this was not going to work. None of the people I knew who had taken these courses were functioning in the prophetic outside of the church and many weren't even functioning in it inside the church! I needed to develop something new.

The new course needed to be built on an apostolic foundation.[5] It also needed to be holistic in its approach, since prophecy is not just for inside the walls of the church. It is meant to impact the whole world! Prophecy also needs to become practical so that we can work together with the Holy Spirit to see the things that already exist in heaven—and revealed by prophecy—take shape down here on the earth. I therefore needed to train prophets and prophetic people to be able to work together well with apostles, since apostles generally have the anointing to build.

A quick aside: for the purposes of this book, a "prophet" is someone who functions in the biblical office of the prophet. "Prophetic people" are those who have asked Christ into their lives and, as a result, have the Holy Spirit living within them. Not all believers are called to be prophets, but all of us are called to be prophetic!

We also needed to equip people to be able to effectively prophesy into all aspects of society. With all of the changes taking place around us, many of those working in government, business and the media don't know what to do or how to respond. They need to hear the Lord's voice in their situations. This meant that we needed to teach people about protocol and expose them to opportunities to prophesy in different environments during the training itself. I wanted our students to be able to prophesy with confidence long after the training had ended. Finally, the training needed to be relational and emphasize character as well as anointing. I wanted to see prophetic people raised up who are a blessing to the local churches that they are a part of.

I developed a curriculum that consisted of three schools—level 1, 2 and 3. I decided to call them "Schools of the Prophets" instead of "Prophetic Schools" because I wanted to emphasize the person, not the gift: God has given prophets and prophetic people to the Church. The School of the Prophets 1 emphasizes prophecy in practice and protocol. School 2 emphasizes testing prophetic words and growing in accuracy in the prophetic, and School 3 emphasizes prophecy both inside and outside of the church. School 3 also teaches the students how to establish healthy and stable prophetic teams in churches and regions and how to prophesy into society's different spheres of influence. Some people call these spheres the "Seven Mountains."[6]

I've taught these Schools of the Prophets for several years now and we have received a lot of positive feedback. One of the compliments that has meant the most to me came from a denominational leader in my home nation of the Netherlands. He said: "We always know when people have done your Schools of the Prophets. They prophesy accurately, they are teachable and they are a joy to work with!" As a church leader and a prophet myself, his words were extremely gratifying. We also hear the same things from business leaders and from those who work in government.

I wrote this book in response to the many requests that I've received from those in the English-speaking nations for the Schools of the Prophets in the last few years. It has taken me five years to write, primarily because I am a scientist. I enjoyed studying chemistry at school and eventually wound up getting a Ph.D. in it. I'm also very analytically inclined—and this shapes how I write about prophecy. I share my own journey and the insights that God has given me about the gift of prophecy and about being a prophet in our times of radical change.

Part 1 of this book will help you to understand why prophecy is so important for seeing revival and reformation in our generation. You will learn how to discern God's voice, how to grow in accuracy and confidence in your prophesying, prophetic protocol and how to test your prophetic words.

Today's prophets are no longer just mouthpieces who deliver the message. Our lives need to back up the prophetic words that we deliver to others. This is especially true if God uses us in domains outside of the church. This is the time for the Josephs and Daniels of our generation to stand up. To take the heart of God to the heart of government. So in Part 2, we'll talk about the character required of prophets who want to be used by God in this hour.

Prophecy does not stand on its own. In order for it to flourish it has to be an intrinsic part of the culture of our churches and organizations. In Part 3 of this book you will learn what that culture is, the role that leaders play in shaping it, and how prophecy in turn influences the cultures in which it is embedded. You will also learn how to take revelation from heaven and to put it into practice so that you can see more of the glory of God being revealed in you and through you.

As we begin this voyage of discovery, I pray you will discover more of the depths of who God truly wants to be for you. I also pray that you will learn how to work together with Him through revelation to see God's Kingdom advanced on the earth.

PROPHECY

Prophecy is essential for seeing revival and reformation in our generation. Learn how to discern God's voice, how to grow in accuracy and confidence in your prophesying, prophetic protocol and how to test your prophetic words.

CHAPTER 1

Repositioning the Prophetic

We're living in a time where God is not only changing the Church, He's changing the world, and we have to start to think differently about the role of prophets and the prophetic.

"If you go out that door without praying for him again, things are going to go horribly wrong!" The voice inside my head was insistent. I was just about to leave home to go to church. The voice confirmed to me that something was going on that day that was not normal. Back then my husband, Dick, and I were part of a church-planting initiative. He's a runner, and the day before he had run more than twelve miles and felt great! But the next day I couldn't get him to wake up. I was worried. His skin had an unusual gray color and he couldn't open his eyes. It was also hard to understand him when he talked. He didn't move and could only mumble.

I closed the front door of our house and went back upstairs to our bedroom. I knelt down beside Dick and asked, "Lord Jesus, what do you want me to pray?" Two words came into my mind: "coma" and "deep sleep." These words made no sense to me at all. However, Dick was looking really ill. Unsure of how to pray and feeling more than a little bit silly I said, "Lord Jesus, I ask you to burn coma and deep sleep now with the fire of Your Holy Spirit." Suddenly the gray color left Dick's skin through his feet and disappeared down from the bed into the floor! It looked a lot like something you'd expect to see in an animated film.

Dick had been trying to open his eyes all morning without success. Now his eyes were wide open and he jumped out of bed. He looked at me and said, "I feel great! You go to church and I'll eat, get dressed and follow." We live in Amsterdam and it was a 45-minute bike ride to church. Dick didn't just follow me. He passed me on the way there and arrived before I did! That was the day I discovered how essential it is to hear God's voice and to act on it.

Looking back, I realized that during that first year of church planting Dick had been sick several times. It was always on a Sunday and it always caused him to miss church. We thought that it was a natural reaction to the fact that it had been a busy year. We had just gotten married and moved into a new home. Dick had also changed jobs, and now we were helping to start a new church. It's difficult to walk in your calling as a church leader if you're not even able to be there! What we thought was natural, actually had a spiritual root. And that meant it could only be solved spiritually. We had to learn to actively use the authority we have in Christ for this.

Personal Repositioning

Nothing in my background had prepared me for dealing with the spiritual world in this way. Having become a believer when I was young, I was brought up in a church that did not believe in the spiritual world or in the manifestation of the gifts of the Holy Spirit. I was taught that speaking in tongues was demonic. I will always be grateful for the Bible knowledge that I received while in that church, but I did have to unlearn a lot of things in order to be able to embrace the move of the Holy Spirit. That was not easy.

During my first few years at university I worked for a Christian student organization. We prided ourselves on our knowledge of Scriptures. We memorized the Bible and were convinced that we needed nothing else. However, there was a problem. We saw almost no fruit as a result of all our hard work. We prayed. We fasted. We did outreach. We did everything we knew how to do, and yet almost no lives were changed and no one came to Christ. I wasn't seeing any of the things happen in my life that I read about regularly in the book of Acts.

After a few years I started to get discouraged. I was twenty-five years old at the time and I thought, if I'm this worn out now, what is it going to be like when I'm seventy! It was then that I made a decision that would prove to be life-changing. I decided that I wasn't going to settle for anything less than what God had promised in His Word. I was determined to pray until the things that I read about in the book of Acts became reality in my life. Several times a week I'd go out into the woods around the university campus and cry out to God, begging Him to break me out of my experience and into the new dimension that I so desperately longed for. I prayed this same prayer throughout the four years that I was a Ph.D. student.

That prayer was answered nine years after I started to pray. By that time, I had moved to Amsterdam to work for a large multinational company. I was part of an evangelical church in the city and we were in trouble. The pastor had had to be fired for things that had to do with a lack of integrity and we had tried for months to find a replacement. It didn't matter what we did, nothing worked. In addition to that, nobody wanted to be part of the future leadership team. We were desperate, and Dick and I decided to start to pray regularly about this with some people from the church.

It was 1994 and we had been hearing stories about the out-pouring of the Holy Spirit in Toronto. Some of us were really hungry for it. One night one of the ladies present suggested that we move the tables and chairs in the room to the side while we prayed. No sooner had we started than Dick silently bent forward. To my surprise, his forehead hit the ground with his arms straight out behind him. It was a posture that seemed physically impossible. One of the women started to laugh and another started to cry. I wish I could say that I rejoiced at these unexpected manifestations of the Holy Spirit, but I didn't. I was horrified. I stood there and said, "This can't be God!" and walked out. I had been used to very quiet and orderly church meetings in the past, and the way I saw it what was happening was not orderly. For the rest of the meeting, while the group prayed inside, I walked around outside the church building praying against what was happening inside!

We had these prayer meetings once a week and every time we met, Dick and the others were overcome by the manifestations of the Holy Spirit. And every time I would walk out. Finally, after six weeks of praying outside I heard a quiet voice. It wasn't coming from my head but from my heart, and it said, "But this is Me too." I stopped in my tracks. Somehow I knew that this was God and that He was talking directly to me. There was a bench nearby and I went and sat down. As I did, I heard the voice again: "But this is Me too." And then it hit me—this was what I'd been praying for those four years while doing my Ph.D.!

Even though the voice was quiet I knew that I had a choice to make. I knew in my heart that if I said no to this, God wouldn't love me any less. But I also knew that saying no would close the door to Him being able to answer my prayer. I started to cry. Finally I prayed, "Lord, You know that I'm afraid, but I say 'yes' to You. I want You and I say yes to all of You, even the parts that I'm not comfortable with."

After sitting for a while, I got up and went back inside to the prayer meeting. Again, Dick was there bent forward with his forehead on the ground and again, the others were laughing, crying or just sitting quietly enjoying the presence of the Holy Spirit. I still felt uncomfortable, but things were now settled in my heart.

It would still take me another few years to get comfortable with these types of manifestations of the Holy Spirit. I had so many things to unlearn. Years later, I realized that in addition to my theology, one of the other reasons why I had felt so uncomfortable back then was because I had areas of emotional pain in my heart that still needed to be healed. When the Holy Spirit turns up He tends to put His finger on these areas, and that can be scary if you've been used to putting a lid on your emotions. The Holy Spirit, however, wanted to heal my emotions.

That choice was a turning point in my life. My "yes" allowed God to open up the realm of the supernatural to me in a way that has exceeded all my expectations. My faith is no longer boring but has become an adventure, and these days God's presence, the supernatural, and especially hearing God's voice in prophecy, have become normal parts of my daily experience, often with surprising results.

Prophetic Personalities

Christians often view prophets in one of two main ways.

The first is that prophets are well-meaning daydreamers who use vague or completely incomprehensible language when they prophesy. I've actually spoken to people who really believe that if you can understand a word then it can't be prophetic! This kind of prophecy is not uncommon. The words spoken have some ability to encourage others and in that sense they are valuable. However, they often have no relationship to the real world and therefore no significant ability to impact our lives or our societies.

The second is that modern-day prophets are the successors of the Old Testament ones; they function according to the Old Testament paradigm. Prophets and prophetic people who view things this way are often angry and their words are sharp and judgmental. Needless to say, their prophetic words are not encouraging. This group makes people want to turn around and run the other way when they see them coming. After a few encounters, churches usually don't want to have anything to do with them or the prophetic. Thankfully, modern-day prophets like Graham Cooke, Shawn Bolz, Kris Vallotton and others have pinpointed this problem and are teaching modern-day prophets how to prophesy based on love, not condemnation.

The truth is that there is no one specific type of prophetic personality. Jesus said, "My sheep hear my voice, and I know them, and they follow me" (John 10:27). What I particularly love about this verse is what it doesn't say. It doesn't say "My *charismatic* sheep hear My voice" or "My *creative, off-the-wall, prophetic* sheep hear My voice." No, *all* God's sheep are able to hear and recognize His voice. If the Holy Spirit lives in you, you qualify. God's people are supposed to be prophetic.

The fact that God would use me to teach others how to hear His voice is a reminder to me that He has a sense of humor. I'm nothing like what I, or others, used to think that prophets were like. A few years ago, at the end of one of our Schools of the Prophets a man came up to me. He said, "I'd like to thank you for this school. I really enjoyed it. I have to confess that I signed up so that I could understand my wife better. She's prophetic and I often just don't get her. However, I got more than I bargained for. I learned how to prophesy and discovered that I'm prophetic too!"

He then whispered something that made me want to laugh and cry at the same time. "It took me the first three lessons before I realized that you were the teacher!"

I whispered back, "The fact that I was standing in front of the class teaching didn't give you a hint?"

He said, "No, I saw you standing there teaching but I kept expecting the real teacher to come out—a smelly old man with long grey hair and a flower-power T-shirt. You're nothing like that. You've got a Ph.D. in chemistry, you're beautiful and intelligent." My ego was being stroked when he said that, until I thought about what he was comparing me to! "You can think logically and you're prophetic. I'm an accountant and I always thought that accountants couldn't be prophetic. You taught me this wasn't true!" One of the things I hope to emphasize in this book is that we, the Church, really need to understand this.

Why is Prophecy Needed?

God is changing more than the Church. He is changing the world. In a recent article in a Dutch national newspaper, Dr. Paul Kennedy, a Yale University professor who studies the dynamics of social change, wrote that the age we now live in is unparalleled in the history of civilization. There are forces currently at work that are transforming the world so thoroughly that if we were able to be transported thirty years into the future, we would not be able to recognize it.[7] He goes on to say that we are living in a watershed moment in history, the likes of which has not been seen since the Protestant Reformation. No one living in 1480 would have recognized the world fifty years later, in 1530. New nation states had been formed, Christianity had been divided, European explorers were colonizing North and South America and the Gutenberg Press was revolutionizing communication.

Today, in addition to massive technological advances, there are equally significant economic and geopolitical shifts affecting our world. The US dollar is no longer the undisputed king of the international currencies and Brexit (as I write this book it is still being negotiated) is pushing the European Union to breaking point. Military spending in Asia is skyrocketing, and the United Nations and NATO are becoming increasingly ineffective as China and Russia regularly veto motions by the US and vice versa. All of these things show that we have entered a new era. The only thing that we can say with certainty is that "we have never been this way before."

In the midst of this turmoil, God is raising up his prophets. Instead of being on the edge of the Church and society, He is calling us to be present in the midst of both of them. This idea isn't new. It's as old as the Scriptures themselves.

In 2 Chronicles 20 we find the story of King Jehoshaphat. Three armies had come to fight against him and his nation, Judah. When he heard this, he was terrified and begged the Lord for guidance. He also commanded everyone in Judah to begin fasting. On a specific day, people from all the towns of Judah and Jerusalem came to seek the Lord's help. After Jehoshaphat prayed, the Spirit of the Lord (the Holy Spirit) fell upon Jahaziel, who was standing in the crowd. He said, "Listen, all Judah and inhabitants of Jerusalem and King Jehoshaphat: Thus says the LORD to you, 'Do not be afraid and do not be dismayed at this great horde, for the battle is not yours but God's . . . You will not need to fight in this battle. Stand firm, hold your position, and see the salvation of the LORD on your behalf, O Judah and Jerusalem.' Do not be afraid and do not be dismayed. Tomorrow go out against them, and the LORD will be with you" (2 Chron. 20:15, 17).

Jahaziel came from a long line of prophets, and his ancestor Asaph had been a Levite and one of the writers of the Psalms. There must have been many prophets in the crowd that day, but the Holy Spirit chose him to deliver the message to the king and the people. I've often wondered why. Maybe one of the main reasons for this was that Jahaziel was well known. He and his family were well known. His life and character were known, in addition to his prophetic accuracy. The survival of the entire nation hinged on it obeying God's instructions. God needed his message to be delivered by someone the people knew and could trust. The next day, as the people went out to meet the enemy the king said,

"Believe in the LORD your God, and you will be established; believe his prophets, and you will succeed" (2 Chron. 20:20). That's how much confidence the king had in the prophetic word that Jahaziel delivered to him and his people.

We Have to Think Differently

For years now, many of us have heard that we have to think big. But that's no longer enough. We have to start to think differently. In 2011 the Elijah List (a website with publications of current prophetic words) published a prophetic word of mine that I had released through the Netherlands Prophetic Council. In it I wrote:

> In our current paradigm we still make a distinction between those with a kingly anointing (marketplace ministers—those called to work outside of the area of full-time Christian ministry) and those with a priestly (full-time ministry) anointing; between those who are called to pray and those who are called to go and to do. This dividing line will be blown to bits as God raises up a new breed—the 'Priest Kings.' They will be those called to both pray and to do. Jesus is our example:

> Then he will receive royal honor and will rule as king from his throne. He will also serve as priest from his throne, and there will be perfect harmony between his two roles.
> – ZECHARIAH 6:13 (NLT)

> Apostles and prophets will be raised up who have the wisdom, strategy and grace to mentor and disciple people who can lead corporations as CEOs, entrepreneurs, heads of communities, states and even nations. Apostles and prophets will not just plant and build churches, but they will have the structures for managing and rebuilding ruined cities and nations. Prophets will serve in government, helping to structure the educational policy of nations, etc.

> The year 2012 will mark the beginning of the Church's finest hour. While the world sinks into panic as the economic crisis worsens globally and great societal unrest is unleashed, the Church, with the new breed of priest-king in place, will shine and finally be able to walk in the Kingdom authority and power that God has always intended.[8]

When God gives you this kind of a prophetic word, He will usually use you to help fulfill it. In 2016 Stacey Campbell, a senior prophetic minister and a dear friend, asked me and another person to join her in organizing a meeting of thirty key leaders for Europe in the areas of revival, prayer and fasting and reformation. I was in charge of inviting those who God is using to bring reformation. Those I invited to speak had been speakers at Economic Summit meetings in the past.

Graham Power, founder and CEO of Unashamedly Ethical and founder of the Global Day of Prayer, started things off. He explained how the Global Day of Prayer started when God gave him a prophetic dream. In this dream he saw three ocean waves hitting the earth. The first was a wave of prayer and fasting. The second was the Marketplace Movement[9] and the third was the great harvest of souls. This dream made a powerful impression on Graham and he prayed that if it was from God, He would give him the same dream a second time.

Sure enough, He did. Since Graham was now certain that his dream was from God, he knew that he needed to act. He reasoned: if the first wave is a wave of prayer and fasting, he needed to at least organize a prayer meeting. After praying and talking to friends he decided to rent the Newlands Rugby Stadium in Cape Town. Normally speaking, private individuals or groups are not allowed to rent the stadium due to the large demand. God's intervention allowed them to get the permit to use the stadium, the funds to pay for it and for the meeting, and even to see the weather change on the day of the meeting itself. Amazingly, 45,000 people came to that first meeting! Graham went on to tell us that the prayer movement expanded and grew, so that a number of years later, 300 million people prayed on five continents across the earth! When Graham said that, all of a sudden the leaders of the prayer and fasting movements became very quiet. God had used a marketplace minister to ignite something that most of them had not managed to achieve.

The next speaker was John Smith (not his real name). John is a director of the economic think tank of the company that he works for. He's also a brother in Christ and a brilliant economist. John told us that when he was in his teens he wanted go to seminary and study to become a full-time minister. God spoke to him, however, and said, "No! I don't want you to go to seminary. I want you to be like a Daniel in Babylon." It was then that John decided to study economics.

In 2007 the CEO of his company asked John and his team to come up with an answer to the question, "What is the right level of profit for the company?" It's very interesting and significant that this question came from a business leader. Why? Because business leaders never ask this question!

His company is a family owned business and one of the largest multinational corporations in the world. It is not a Christian company, but the original founder was a man of faith, and around the time that the CEO asked John the question they found a document that echoed the CEO's question. It was an old, yellowed document, written by the company's founder. It was addressed to the company directors and said, "The company's objective is the manufacture and distribution of food products in such manner as to promote a mutuality of services and benefits among: consumers, distributors, competitors, our direct suppliers of goods and services, governmental bodies, all employees of the company and its shareholders. This expresses the total purpose for which the company exists—nothing less—and it is expected that the Board of Directors, all management and employees of the company, will be motivated by this basic objective, and will keep it constantly in mind as the guiding principle in all their work for the company."[10] Talking about divinely orchestrated circumstances!

John went away to think and to pray about the question. Later, in his next meeting with the CEO, he wrote on a whiteboard what he felt was the right strategy. Astonished, the CEO pulled a crumpled piece of paper out of his pocket and showed it to John. He said, "I had a dream a few years ago and felt that it must mean something. This is what I saw ..." When John looked at the paper he saw the same thing that he himself had just written on the whiteboard!

John ended his talk by saying, "It's like we're living in the days of Daniel and Nebuchadnezzar all over again. Kings and rulers are having dreams. God is showing His people what these dreams are and He's giving them the ability to interpret them so that these leaders know what to do."

The final speaker in the meeting's section on the reformation of society was Jan Sturesson. Jan is the CEO of RESTING, a consultancy that advises governments and businesses. He is also the Director of the International Christian Chamber of Commerce. Jan talked about several instances where He needed to rely on hearing God's voice in his positions at the World Bank, the European Commission and the World Economic Forum. A few years ago, Jan was in Amsterdam. He'd been invited by the mayor of the city to provide advice on how to position Amsterdam as a city of the future. The mayor and the city councilors also wanted to know what they needed to focus on in order to achieve this. Jan prayed, asked the Holy Spirit for revelation and then wrote down his thoughts. He submitted his recommendations to the mayor and his staff. A few weeks later, they came back to him and said, "We don't know where you're getting your ideas from, but they are ten times better than the ideas of any of the other consultants who we also invited to submit ideas."

Jan also told us about several instances when, after consulting sessions, he would go out to dinner with these leaders. Time and again God would give him prophetic insight into their personal situations, and he would then be able to share the love of Christ with them and to pray. As a result, several of them had accepted the Lord.

When Graham, John and Jan finished you could have heard a pin drop in the room. The audience didn't know what to say. Finally, one of them whispered, "I've never heard anything like this before!" Graham, John, Jan and many others are a lot like Joseph and Daniel. Joseph and Daniel were not full-time ministers. They were civil servants who could hear God's voice. However, that was not why they were promoted. What distinguished these men was that they also operated in the spirit of wisdom. They were not only able to receive revelation, but they knew what to do with it. Wisdom helps us to take the revelation that God gives us and to make it practical. This is crucial.

God's Voice and God's Kingdom

Why is it so important that we learn to hear God's voice? One of the reasons is because that it is one of the main ways that God's Kingdom and His glory become visible on the earth.

When Jesus taught His disciples to pray, He said, "When you pray, say: Our Father in heaven, hallowed be Your name. Your kingdom come. Your will be done on earth as it is in heaven" (Luke 11:2, NKJV). Another way to express what Jesus taught us to pray is, "May Your Kingdom come *because* Your will is being done on earth as it is in heaven." A kingdom is the domain of a king. It is a place where the will of the king is being done; where his rule and reign are visible. How do we know what God's will is? By reading His Word and by hearing and obeying His voice. As we do God's will, His Kingdom is demonstrated on earth through signs, wonders and miracles; through healing sick bodies, families, societies, institutions and nations. Being able to hear the voice of God is the starting point.

When Jesus asked His disciples who people said He was, and then who they said He was, it was a milestone moment when Peter said, "You are the Christ, the Son of the living God" (Matt. 16:16). This was one of the first times since Jesus had been on the earth that anyone had received prophetic revelation directly from God: "flesh and blood has not revealed this to you, but my Father who is in heaven" (Matt. 16:17). Jesus then says, "I will build my church, and the gates of hell shall not prevail against it. I will give you the keys of the kingdom of heaven, and whatever you bind on earth shall be bound in heaven, and whatever you loose on earth shall be loosed in heaven" (Matt. 16:18–19).

If you were raised a Roman Catholic, you would have been taught that Peter is the rock upon which Christ will build His Church. If you were raised a Protestant you would have been taught that "the rock" that Jesus is talking about is the revelation that Jesus Christ is the Son of God, the Messiah. While this is true, there is also a third option—that Jesus is actually saying that now that we, His children, can hear His voice, He can build His Church and the gates of hell will not be able to prevail against it! Hearing God's voice is essential for the advance of the Church, the Kingdom and God's people!

CHAPTER 2

God Talk

"There is more!" No matter how much we think we know about God and His ways, there is always more. It's the same with prophecy. While the gift of prophecy manifests itself in the form of encouragement, comfort and words that build us up, there is more.

When God speaks things happen. They always have. When God spoke our world and the universe were created, kingdoms fell, societies were saved and armies destroyed. If the Bible teaches anything, it is that you can expect things to happen when God talks (Isa. 55:11). God speaks through both prophecy and the Scriptures, but they are different. The Scriptures contain God's revelation for all people groups everywhere, at all times. Prophecy is God's specific revelation for individuals, or groups, in specific situations, at specific times. It is conditional and requires, among other things, obedience in order for it to be fulfilled. Since God does speak through prophecy, it is normal to expect that things should happen when we prophesy.

The Lord Jesus has been really kind to me, and during the past few years I've had the joy of seeing many of the prophetic words that I've spoken out over others being fulfilled. It's become almost a weekly occurrence to hear the testimonies of those who I've prophesied over. Naturally, it's encouraging for them, but it's also extremely fulfilling for me. I love to see people realizing that God knows them so intimately and loves them so much that He would send someone to prophesy over them and then fulfill His word!

I did not grow up in a church where people believed in prophecy. Looking back, however, I realize that there were clues that I might be prophetic. First, when I was a child my parents and I thought that I had an overactive imagination. I saw all sorts of things moving around in my room at night and often had vivid dreams that I would remember the next morning. Unfortunately, many of these dreams were nightmares. Back then I didn't realize that what I thought was my imagination was actually things that I was seeing in the spiritual realm. Second, I also loved to pray, and often when praying for others they would say to me, "How did you know that?" I, of course, didn't have a clue.

The first time that I can remember consciously recognizing the sound of God's voice was as an adult, after I'd moved to Amsterdam. I was part of a small Bible study group in my church, and that night the leader of the group said that we were going to practice "hearing God's voice." He prayed and then told us to wait in silence for five minutes. For the majority of those five minutes I heard absolutely nothing. My mind was completely blank. Every once in a while I would have a thought, "He loves us." "These are just my own thoughts," I reasoned. "Of course God loves us! It's in the Bible." When the five minutes were up the group leader asked us to share what we had heard. To my surprise, five out of the eleven of us had heard exactly the same thing! That was the first time that I realized that the voice of God often sounds like our own thoughts!

The key, however, is that these thoughts are spontaneous. They are things that we were not actively thinking about before. Spontaneous thoughts are often the voice of the spiritual world. God will frequently speak like this, even when people don't believe you can hear God's voice for yourself. I've heard many people say things like, "I wasn't sure what to do, but after I prayed I had an idea." Most of the time these are businesspeople who don't always believe that the gifts of the Holy Spirit are for today and who certainly do not consider themselves to be prophetic!

Recognizing God

How do you know when it's God talking? God's thoughts are usually much wiser and more loving than our own. I've lost count of the number of meetings that I've been in where I had to talk to people about unpleasant things. Each time I'd prepare myself well so that I knew what I was going to say. Things would go according to plan until I prayed at the start of these meetings. Then I would hear myself saying things that I hadn't planned on saying. Each time God would give the right words and the right insights. I'd often be amazed at what I heard myself saying because I knew that I didn't have that kind of wisdom. And the outcome was often much better than I could have brought about myself.

While spontaneous thoughts are the way the spiritual world speaks to us, not all of our spontaneous thoughts come from God's Holy Spirit. That's why it's so important for us to let God transform us into new people by changing the way we think (Rom 12:2). Jesus left no doubt about it when He said that a good tree cannot produce bad fruit and a bad tree cannot produce good fruit (Matt. 7:18). Therefore, we can and should expect thoughts from the Holy Spirit to produce the fruit of the Spirit in our lives: "love, joy, peace, patience, kindness, goodness, faithfulness, gentleness [and] self-control" (Gal. 5:22–23). If our thoughts and words produce the opposite, like fear or hatred, they are not from the Holy Spirit.

We never have to worry about not being able to hear God's voice. This is because He is always talking:

> How precious to me are your thoughts, O God! How vast is the
> sum of them! If I would count them, they are more than the sand.
> I awake, and I am still with you.
> – PSALM 139:17–18

If God thinks about us more than the number of grains of
sand, then He never stops thinking or talking about us.
It's like having a radio. When the radio is turned off, we
don't hear anything. Just because we don't hear anything it
doesn't mean that the radio stations are not broadcasting.
It just means that we need to turn on the radio and tune in
to the right channel. If you tune in to what God is saying
you can always prophesy.

Prophecy

Prophecy is the divinely inspired ability to receive messages
from God's Holy Spirit and to communicate them to others.
These messages reveal God's heart, mind and will for the
people and the world around us. In other words, prophecy
is speaking out the words that God gives us. I used to think
that if you didn't get the gift of prophecy when you were
born again you were never going to get it. The apostle Paul's
words, "Pursue love, and earnestly desire the spiritual gifts,
especially that you may prophesy" (1 Cor. 14:1) have caused
me to think again. They mean that if you don't think you
have the gift of prophecy yet, you can ask for it. His words
should encourage us: if you get nothing else, make sure that
you get the gift of prophecy. Why do we need this gift so
much? Because prophecy is meant to encourage, comfort
and to build us up (1 Cor. 14:3).

A few years ago I was part of the team planning a pan-
European meeting bringing together the leaders of international prayer and missions organizations. The meeting
was interdenominational and the leaders of the organization

had decided that in order to keep the peace they would prohibit open manifestations of the Holy Spirit, including prophecy. I was responsible for inviting speakers who were having an impact in society. They were going to tell what God was doing through them and their organizations. I decided to invite Dr. Sharon Stone, a friend of mine who is a well-respected prophet internationally and who had played an important role in seeing the constitution of Romania changed.

Her story about how this happened was impressive. She had been invited to Romania to preach. One day, a child who lived on the streets had stolen some food to eat and the police had caught him. At that specific moment my friend walked by. She stopped and looked on in horror as one of the policemen took the cigarette that he was smoking and pressed it into the skin on the child's shoulder. Enraged, my friend screamed at him to stop. He just looked at her and laughed. After he had burned the child several times, the policemen let the boy go.

When Sharon reported it to the local Chief of Police he said, "Lady, street children are not protected by our constitution. What are you going to do about it? Change the constitution?"

She reacted and said, "Yes! If that's what it takes." It took her several years and quite a lot of her own money, but she eventually accomplished it.

In the telephone calls I had with her to help her prepare for the meeting I said, "Share your story but do not prophesy."

On the day she was scheduled to speak, she stood up and looked around the room. She opened her mouth to start speaking and then shut it. She did this again twice. Finally, she looked at the audience, sighed, and said, "I know that Arleen and the organizers have asked me not to prophesy ... but the Lord keeps telling me do it. So I have decided to prophesy." She then proceeded to speak out prophetic words of encouragement for three of the leaders in the room.

The whole time she was prophesying I sat there thinking that this would be a good moment for a hole to open up in the ground under me so that I could disappear into it. After she finished, she sat down. She looked at me and just shrugged. Within two minutes of the end of her session a long line of people had formed. I thought that they were there to complain. They weren't. Many of them had tears in their eyes. They looked at me and said, "Could you please ask her to pray for us like she prayed for those people during her talk? We have worked so hard and are so tired. We need encouragement too!"

That day I learned an important lesson. Never again would I allow myself to quench the work of the Holy Spirit by cooperating with those who forbid people to prophesy. I repented deeply before God for this. We, the planning committee, didn't know it at the time, but that was exactly what the participants needed. They needed the clear expression of God's love for them through a personal prophetic word.

Encourage, Comfort, Strengthen

Prophetic words offering encouragement, comfort, or that build us up are tremendously important. Prophetic words like these can help us to persevere when things get rough. I have experienced this myself.

Within two weeks of arriving in Amsterdam to start my new job at a multinational corporation I got a telephone call from my mother in Canada. She called to wish me a happy birthday and to tell me that she was seriously ill. She'd been diagnosed the day before with an aggressive form of leukemia and needed to start chemotherapy immediately. What we didn't know back then is that she would pass away less than a year later.

In the eleven months before she died, Mom went through three rounds of chemotherapy. With each treatment she bled internally and I would get a phone call telling me that if I wanted to see her alive I would have to come immediately. I spent a lot of time that year on emergency flights between Amsterdam and Toronto. Naturally, I wanted to be close to my mother. But every time I told her I wanted to quit my job and come back home she said, "Don't even think about it! You're right where God wants you to be. I want you to walk in God's will for your life." Ten days after I'd returned to the Netherlands following her third round of chemotherapy, she took a turn for the worse and I had to return to Canada again.

Even though my family and I and others had prayed for her healing many times, she had not been healed. I still remember praying during that flight home and asking God to either heal her quickly or take her home to heaven quickly. My family and I had spent nights with her in the hospital and we had heard the screams of those who were in tremendous pain, even though they had been given morphine. My mom knew Christ as her Savior and I didn't want to see her suffer anymore. Four days later she went to be with the Lord.

The burial was difficult and glorious at the same time. Mom had asked me to speak at her funeral. She said, "I know where I'm going but Arleen, there are so many who don't know Jesus. I want you to preach the gospel to them and tell them how to be saved." I did, and that day twelve women gave their lives to the Lord! After the funeral I talked to them. Their stories were all very similar. They said things like, "When I was a teenager I got pregnant. My parents threw me out of the house and didn't want to have anything to do with me or the baby. Sometimes things were really hard and I didn't have enough money to buy diapers or baby food. It was always when I was at my lowest point that I'd hear a knock at the door and there would be your mother standing there with the things that I needed. She would say,

'I just wanted to stop by to see if you were okay.'" My father, my sister and I were shocked! My mother was a nurse on the maternity ward at the hospital, but she had never told us anything about what she had done. She allowed herself to be led by the Holy Spirit to show God's love to these women when they needed it the most. Needless to say, their stories comforted us and encouraged us in ways that we could never have imagined.

Her death also had a huge impact on my priorities. I was following God, but I was also really ambitious. I loved my mother, but could never understand why she kept turning down the promotions that she was offered at work. In total she turned down six promotions. On the day of her funeral 600 people crowded into the church to attend her funeral. The hospital where she worked even gave all non-essential personnel the day off so that they could attend. This was the first time in the history of that hospital that they had ever done this. Hearing the stories of all those women who she had helped and seeing all of the others who she had blessed in her life, I finally understood why she turned down those promotions. To her, contact with her patients was more important than a higher salary and a desk job. Right then I realized that even if I reached CEO level in the company I was working for, my life would not have the same impact that hers did if I kept going the way I was. Burying a loved one really causes you to recognize what's truly important.

After the funeral I returned to Amsterdam. Even with the encouragement that these stories offered, the world had changed for me. Try as I might, I could not get past the heartache of her not being there anymore. She was my best friend, and I felt as if something inside me had died. Because I was either working or flying back and forth to Canada during my first year in Amsterdam, I hadn't really been able to make any close friends there. I was incredibly lonely and I really wanted to go back to Canada.

One Sunday I felt so low that as I cried I prayed and said, "God, do You even see me anymore? I need to know that You are still in control of my life and that You see me. This grief is so heavy that I don't think that I can stay here on my own anymore." That day I decided to go to an evangelical church that I had never been to before. I sat through the service and didn't hear a thing that was said. As the last song was being sung I started to put on my coat to leave early. I didn't feel like talking to anyone and wanted to leave as soon as possible. I had also made a decision. I was going to leave Amsterdam and return to Toronto.

As I was sliding out of the pew, I felt someone put their hand on my shoulder. It was the lady sitting behind me. She said, "Please don't go just yet. I have something that I need to tell you." I was surprised. Waiting was the last thing I wanted to do. However, I did wait, even if it was only to be polite. After the service she introduced herself and said, "I know that this sounds strange and that we don't know each other. During the service I heard the Lord speaking to me about you. He said, 'Tell her that I see her. I want you to tell her that I see her.' Does that mean anything to you?" I will never forget that moment. All of a sudden the crushing weight of grief lifted. God had just let me know through this woman who I had never met before that He saw me and was with me. Since this was true, I knew that He would give me the strength to carry on. I also knew that I really was supposed to be in Amsterdam!

Back then I did not know anything about the prophetic. That one word brought me freedom from the crushing burden of grief I was carrying. I shudder to think what would have happened if that woman had not been obedient to God and had kept the word to herself. Without it, I would almost certainly have gone back to Canada and my life would have taken a very different course. That day I learned a very important lesson about the absolute necessity of having the prophetic operating in and through our lives!

There is More

People who know me know that I love the phrase, "There is more!" No matter how much we think we know about God and His ways, there is always more. It's the same with prophecy. While the gift of prophecy expresses itself in the form of encouragement, comfort and words that build us up, there is more. One of the key reasons why our Schools of the Prophets have had such a positive and unique impact is because we continually encourage our students to go for "the more" that God has for them. This is true of everything we do, including the teaching, the activations and our encouraging them in their walk with God.

I really love to prophesy destiny over people's lives and to give them insight into their gifts, their callings and the processes that God uses in their lives to get them where He wants them to be. I am passionate about this because I am convinced that we only become truly dangerous for the devil and the powers of darkness on the earth when we walk in God's calling for our lives.

Destiny words (words about our gifts and callings) will often take us by surprise and open up new areas that we have never thought about before. It was a normal day for David in the fields tending the sheep. That is, until Samuel came along and anointed him to be the next king of God's people, Israel. From that day onwards the Spirit of God came powerfully upon David and everything was different (1 Sam. 16:13). His circumstances didn't change, but he changed on the inside under the power of the Holy Spirit. When David woke up that morning he had no idea that this would happen, and neither did anybody else who knew him. These inspired words totally changed his sense of destiny and he would never be the same again. This is what destiny words do. They cause us to seriously change what we think we know about ourselves.

An example. Once, when we were busy making the last arrangements for a prophetic conference that we were organizing, I couldn't stop thinking about a man that I had last seen and spoken to several years earlier. After three days of thinking about him I finally sent an SMS message to his daughter to get his mobile phone number and then called him. I said, "John (not his real name), I know that we have not seen each other in a long time, but I'm calling to invite you to the conference that we are planning. I have a strong feeling that God has something special lined up for you and that you need to be there. Will you pray about it and see what He says to you about this?" John said that he would and that he'd get back to me in a few days' time to let me know. In the end he did come.

What I did not know was that when I called him he had been travelling abroad on business. He told me later that he had changed his schedule and rebooked his return flight in order to get back in time for the conference. I talked to him during one of the coffee breaks. During our talk I spoke out a simple prophetic word over him. I said, "John, you are an apostle called to business." All of a sudden he started to cry! This lasted for only a minute, but a minute can seem like a long time when you're standing there watching someone weep and don't know what to do.

When he finally composed himself enough to be able to talk, he said, "For the forty years that I've been a Christian, I have been asking myself what God's plan for me is. I have served as a Christian leader in many different roles and am currently an elder in my local church. But none of this has prevented me from feeling like I was a square peg in a round hole. When you said what you just did, all of a sudden I knew what I was created for. I *am* called to be an apostle in business!" Later that day the speaker also gave him a prophetic word from the stage confirming what I had told him earlier.

That conference had a profound effect on John's life. When he returned to his church he resigned from his position as an elder. He stayed on for a few months until they could find someone else to replace him, and then he left. At the time that John received these words he was the owner of one business that was doing well. In the years that followed, however, he started an additional seven businesses! John was already giving generously to people and to projects that glorified God. But now he sits on the boards of companies that have the ability to finance and initiate things that advance the Kingdom of God in regions and nations!

I have seen similar things happen again and again as I and others have prophesied destiny over people, churches, businesses and other organizations. God says in the Bible, "See, it is I who created the blacksmith who fans the coals into flame and forges a weapon fit for its work" (Isa. 54:16, NIV). In many ways prophetic people are like the blacksmith in this verse. As we speak out the prophetic words of destiny God gives us for people, the fire of God is ignited in their hearts. As they step out and connect with their prophetic destinies they become weapons fit for their work; they are a great threat to the powers of darkness.

CHAPTER 3

Prophets and Prophetic Believers

The words of a prophet have power in the spirit realm and have lasting impact. Their words are able to change the very nature of the person they're prophesying to. You know when you've been in the presence of a true prophet!

I often get asked the question, "When do I know that I'm a prophet?" Even though it shouldn't, this question often causes a lot of controversy in many branches of the Church. This is not an issue for those who don't believe that the spiritual gifts are for today. The tension comes in circles where people do believe that prophecy is for today. We are afraid of people becoming proud, so we call them prophetic instead of prophets. In fact, I have heard leaders of some cutting-edge Church movements say that "we should not get hung up on titles. It is best if we just call everyone prophetic. That way no one can raise themselves above anyone else. God loves everybody the same." Other leaders say, "We do not focus on titles. We focus on function." All of these arguments sound spiritual but there is a problem. If we do not acknowledge both the gift of prophecy and the office of the prophet, we harm the body of Christ as well as the individuals in it.

I'll never forget the day that Stacey Campbell and Dr. Sharon Stone inaugurated the Netherlands Prophetic Council, which I lead. As Stacey was addressing the group, at one point she said, "I want you to repeat after me, 'I am a prophet.'"

It is important to mention here that she was not forcing them to say anything that was not true when she did this. All of the people in the room *were* prophets. There was no doubt about it. What happened next shocked me. Some people started to choke when they tried to talk and three of them dropped to the ground and started to weep. It was not a quiet, polite type of weeping. It was loud and it was messy. The moment they spoke out who they were, deep emotions were released. Almost everyone in the room had suffered for just trying to be who God had made them to be.

This has to change. It is time for us to raise people up and give them the space and the training to function in the fullness of the prophetic ministry in the way that God intended. When we do, we will start to see people's lives changed and our nations shift into alignment with the purposes of God.

Gift and Office

When it comes to the spiritual gifts, love is always our first priority. Let's have another look at 1 Corinthians 14:1, "Pursue love, and earnestly desire the spiritual gifts, especially that you may prophesy." The Greek word for "desire" as it pertains to spiritual gifts actually means to go after them hard. The literal meaning is "to hunt something down until you obtain it." This isn't a suggestion. It's a command. God has always intended for His Church to be prophetic.

The gift of prophecy is given for encouragement, comfort and for building each other up. This is essential, not only in the church, but everywhere. Because it's a gift, prophecy can't be earned or bought (Acts 8:18). As I have said earlier, the great thing is that if you don't think you have the gift of prophecy this verse gives you permission to ask for it! This is a prayer that is definitely in line with God's will.

Many of us don't use the word "office" anymore. For the purposes of this book I will use the word "office" to mean someone who has the gift of prophecy, combined with a clear gift of leadership. It involves having much higher level of authority in the prophetic because the "office" of the prophet is an extension of Jesus Christ's own prophetic ministry (Acts 3:22).

While we can always ask God for the gift of prophecy, Jesus Himself is the One who appoints prophets. In Ephesians Paul writes:

> And he gave the apostles, the prophets, the evangelists, the shepherds and teachers, to equip the saints for the work of ministry, for building up the body of Christ, until we all attain to the unity of the faith and of the knowledge of the Son of God, to mature manhood, to the measure of the stature of the fullness of Christ.
> – EPHESIANS 4:11–13

Together with the other members of the fivefold ministry gifts, prophets are given to equip believers so that they can do what God calls them to do. This is urgent at this time when God is pouring out His Spirit across the earth. We are at the beginning of what many, including me, believe will be the greatest harvest of souls for Jesus that the world has ever seen and the Lord wants to use all of us to make the realm of heaven visible wherever we are. I would even go so far as to say that if you're not being equipped, you need to start to demand it from your church leaders—and if they really don't want to move in that direction, leave and go where you can be equipped. The age of revival and reformation is here and there is no time to waste!

A prophet is someone called by God to speak on His behalf. Prophets can prophesy to encourage, comfort and build people up, but they can also communicate God's will, His direction, revelation, correction and His plans for the future. The ministry of a prophet is more varied and powerful than that of a

Christian who simply prophesies. The words of a prophet have power in the spirit realm and tend to have lasting impact. Their words are able to change the very nature of the person or thing they're prophesying to. You know when you've been in the presence of a true prophet!

The words of a prophet have a different effect on our lives than a sermon. Back in 2008 Sharon Stone came to speak at a prophetic conference our church was hosting in Amsterdam. We were used to having prophetic speakers, but this was one of the first times that we'd heard a prophet of the Lord, someone with the office of a prophet, speak. She prophesied over many of us. We received the faith that we needed for the fulfillment of her words along with the words themselves. That was ten years ago, and to this day people come up to me regularly and say, "The word that Sharon spoke out over me has literally changed my life!" You don't get this to the same degree with a sermon.

I remember one of the very first words that Sharon spoke out over our church back then. It was summer, but when she prophesied she started by saying that she had heard the angels singing Christmas carols as she woke up that morning. There was joy in the atmosphere. She then looked at us and said, "Dick and Arleen, God says that you're pregnant with octuplets! In fact, you're not pregnant any longer. They're here and it's too late to say, 'Can we afford them?' or 'Maybe this wasn't such a good idea after all.' Like it or not, they're here!"

I'd forgotten about that word until recently, when the Lord told me to reread all of the words that had been spoken out over the church by the prophets that have come to us over the years. As I reread this one I had to smile. I still remembered the shock and awe that I felt when she delivered it. Dick and I often say to people these days when we introduce ourselves that "we start things." That's what we do. We start things that grow into ministries and businesses that have a national and international impact. One year we made a resolution not to start anything else because we were already very busy. We didn't manage to keep that resolution, however. That year we ended up having to start a publishing house, Mandate Publishing, in order to translate and publish books on the Courts of Heaven by, among others, Robert Henderson.

In 2018 so many things had been birthed that we needed to find a way to explain to new church members how they were all related to each other. After a whole day of worshiping and waiting on the Lord for insight I remembered Sharon's word. I stood up and drew an octagon on the whiteboard in the room and put the name of one of the entities on each of the sides of the octagon. I started to laugh when I realized that there were eight of them! God had indeed given us octuplets and together these make up the model for our apostolic center in Amsterdam.[11]

Knowing You Are a Prophet

So when *do* you know that you're prophet? You might find it surprising to learn that it's not when someone comes along and prophesies that you are called to be a prophet. This kind of destiny word speaks to the potential that God has placed in you but that may not be a visible reality in your life yet. At a conference, prophetic teacher Lance Wallnau once explained it like this: "Through prophecy, God shows us our face in the future. He does this to sustain us while he shapes our characters so that He can take us to where He's prophesied that He wants us to be."

But we are linear thinkers. That means if someone comes along and prophesies over us, "God has called you to be a great evangelist!" we think, "Move over, Daniel Kolenda, here I come!" God, however, looks at us and says, "Oh, yes, that's the potential that I've placed in you and now I'm going to start to work on you so that I can get you there."

When do you become a prophet? It's when those around you, especially your spiritual leaders, start to acknowledge you as one. Prophets need to have a platform (a place and a people) to prophesy to. If they don't, they'll just be prophesying to the wind and their words won't produce the spiritual fruit that they should.

I had people prophesying over me and telling me that I was "a prophet of the Lord" years before that acknowledgment came from my church and recognized leaders. During this time, I didn't focus on being a prophet. I just focused on trying to bless people by being prophetic and functioning in the gift of prophecy. I was happily prophesying over people when one day Sharon Stone said to me, "Arleen, I think that it's time for me to ordain you and Dick as a prophet and an apostle of the Lord respectively." When you ordain someone, you appoint, anoint and consecrate them for the work of the Lord in a particular position or office. Dick and I were a part of Sharon's network, Christian International Europe, and she had seen how we functioned. She also knew us well and had seen how God had developed both our gifting and our characters throughout the years.

The day that I was ordained she laid hands on my head, anointed me with oil and said, "Arleen, today I ordain you as a prophet of the Lord to your nation, to the nations and to your own home church." I was glad she added those last words, because it made my role in church very clear as well. As she laid her hands on me, she also prophesied that God would give me the ability to discern the thoughts and the intents of people's hearts. That word put the fear of God into me. It's one thing to see people's actions and love them anyway. It's something totally different to see the junk in their hearts, to know what they're really thinking deep down and to keep loving them and praying for them.

The following table explains the difference between the gift of prophecy and the office of the prophet.[12]

THE GIFT OF PROPHECY	THE OFFICE OF THE PROPHET
One of the nine manifestations of the Holy Spirit (1 Cor. 12; 14)	An extension of Jesus, the Prophet (Acts 3:22)
A gift: cannot be bought or sold (Acts 8:18–20) and is not based on our level of maturity	Involves a higher level of spiritual authority for leadership (1 Cor. 12:28)
All believers can ask for it (1 Cor. 14:1)	Jesus chooses the prophet (Eph. 4:11; 1 Cor. 12:29)
Given for comfort, encourage and build us up (1 Cor. 14:3)	Same, plus correction and direction (Ezek. 3:18; 2 Kings 5:10)
Given to serve the Church (1 Peter 4:10)	Given to lay the foundation of the Church and equip the people to serve in the church and in the world (Eph. 2:20; 4:12)
Speaks out gifts and callings	Anoints, imparts and confirms gifts and callings (1 Sam. 10:1; 1 Tim. 4:14; Ex. 28:41; 1 Kings 19:16)
Involves revelation of the past and present (1 Cor. 12:8–10)	Involves revelation of the past, present and future (Acts 11:28; 21:10–11)
Delivers the prophetic word (1 Cor. 14:12)	The lives of prophets back up the words they are called to give (Agabus, Isaiah, Hosea)
Speaks to the Church (1 Cor. 14:2–4)	Speaks to the past, present and future Church, and to social, political, economic and geological arenas (Nahum, Hosea, Obadiah, Elijah, Daniel, Agabus)
Speaks of God's grace (1 Cor. 14:1)	Speaks of God's grace and judgment

Ordination

Ordination raised my level of prophetic accuracy almost immediately. It was as if the flash of a camera had gone off and I could see past, present and future all at the same time. My prophesying was good before, but being ordained took it to a whole different level. A biblical example of what takes place can be seen in Timothy's life. He receives a gift by prophecy and the laying on of hands. The apostle Paul writes to him, "Do not neglect the gift you have, which was given you by prophecy when the council of elders laid their hands on you" (1 Tim 4:14). In the same way, a prophet can also impart a higher level of anointing through the laying on of hands.

To have the "office" of the prophet, apostle, pastor, teacher or evangelist means that you receive God's grace to lead in these areas. A few years ago Gillis Overbeeke, one of my fellow teachers and trainers in our Schools of the Prophets, asked if Dick and I would ordain him as a prophet in the church. Even though we had been ordained, the thought of ordaining someone ourselves was new to us. It took us almost a year to decide to do it. There were no doubts regarding his character or calling, but together with our church's leadership team we needed time to establish the protocol: when to ordain people, who to ordain and how to present this to the congregation. We needed to determine what the ordained person's position in church would be after ordination. We took Gillis' request as a test case.

The first thing we looked at was *who* to ordain. Gillis and I had been teaching the Schools of the Prophets together since 2012. When he asked for ordination in 2016, Gillis and I had worked through many issues. Our personalities are very different and we had different views on several theological points. In the beginning we didn't always agree on the theological foundations that I had adopted for the schools. We took the time to talk about these things and to search the Scriptures together. The theology did not usually change. It was not because I was stubborn (even though I can be sometimes) but because the Holy Spirit was revealing something new which Gillis had to work through. However, I did change my position a few times because of his words. As the proverb says, "You use steel to sharpen steel, and one friend sharpens another" (Prov. 27:17, MSG). We sharpened each other and our schools benefited.

Another argument in favor of ordaining him was that we had seen how he had handled conflicts and were impressed. He did not give up on people. He didn't speak negatively about them to others and he didn't fight to prove he was right. Most of the time he just prayed and the Holy Spirit would open the door for reconciliation. I have great respect for his maturity and the high level of character that he displays on a daily basis. He actively seeks out accountability partners and is respected in church.

The second thing we looked at was *when* to ordain people. This wasn't just about Gillis. We made the decision that we would ordain people who are already serving the body of Christ in a sphere that is broader than just the local church and who function at a consistently high level in the gifting that they have received. Through the years I had seen Gillis grow in accuracy in his prophetic gift and I was hearing the people who he ministered to regularly talk about this. When we asked Gillis why he wanted to be ordained now he said he knew that God had spoken to him about carrying more responsibility for the prophetic in our church. He also knew that he had a role to play as a prophet in the nation. He felt that the impartation that comes with ordination would help him to better fulfill God's call on his life.

Finally, we considered what Gillis' role in the church would be after his ordination. When we had talked to him and prayed for him we decided that he would take on more responsibilities for the training and developing of the prophetic in the church. He is not a part of the leadership team. He does, however, have a high level of maturity and a proven track record of accuracy that allows us to run things by him in order to get his take on what he feels that God is saying.

On the day that he was ordained, Gillis, Dick and I let the church know about the process that we had been through to get to this point. You could hear a sigh of anticipation when we said we hoped that many others would follow. Ordination is not something exclusive. We hoped that Gillis would be the first of many others that we would be able to ordain.

We don't only want to ordain prophets, but also apostles, pastors, teachers and evangelists. A little less than a year after he was ordained, we had a visiting guest speaker in our church from the USA. At lunch after the service he told Dick and I that the prophet in our church had had a word for him that had really encouraged him. He needed to make an important decision when he returned home. Gillis didn't know about that, but he had prophesied and now the guest speaker knew which decision he had to make. That was a special moment for me. Up until that time I had always been "the prophet" in the church. Now I had company.

Whether you as church leader and your church decide to ordain people or not, our role as leaders is to acknowledge the gifts that God has given to people and to help them to cultivate them so that everybody grows.

CHAPTER 4

Dreams and Visions

The pharaohs and the kings of this earth are receiving God-given dreams again. We need to take these dreams seriously and know what to do with them.

When discussing how God speaks, we cannot ignore dreams and visions. "And in the last days it shall be, God declares, that I will pour out my Spirit on all flesh, and your sons and your daughters shall prophesy, and your young men shall see visions, and your old men shall dream dreams; even on my male servants and female servants in those days I will pour out my Spirit, and they shall prophesy" (Acts 2:17–18). This verse does not mean that only young men will see visions and that only old men will prophesy. The Greek and Hebrew sources are richer than our translation, as they show that every single one of God's servants, from young to old, will see visions and dream dreams. In fact, dreams and visions make up almost one-third of the Bible! In this chapter I will focus on a few things that I think are most important.

Do you recall John Smith and his CEO's dream (Chapter 1)? When John's presentation gave both the dream and the strategy to accomplish it, God's power was unleashed. Dreams and visions are important because the pharaohs and the kings of this earth are receiving God-given dreams again. We need to take these dreams seriously and know what to do with them.

The Bible is full of examples of God communicating important things to people through dreams and visions. In the Old Testament, He announced the birth of the Jewish people through a dream. "After these things the word of the LORD came to Abram in a vision: 'Fear not, Abram, I am your shield; your reward shall be very great.' And he brought him outside and said, 'Look toward heaven, and number the stars, if you are able to number them.' Then he said to him, 'So shall your offspring be'" (Gen. 15:1, 5). God also revealed himself to Jacob in a dream: "Jacob left Beersheba and went toward Haran. And he came to a certain place and stayed there that night, because the sun had set. Taking one of the stones of the place, he put it under his head and lay down in that place to sleep. And he dreamed, and behold, there was a ladder set up on the earth, and the top of it reached to heaven. And behold, the angels of God were ascending and descending on it! And behold, the LORD stood above it and said, 'I am the LORD, the God of Abraham your father and the God of Isaac. The land on which you lie I will give to you and to your offspring.'" (Gen. 28:10–13). God even gave Solomon the great wisdom that he is known for through a dream: "That night the LORD appeared to Solomon in a dream, and God said, 'What do you want? Ask, and I will give it to you!'" (1 Kings 3:5, NLT).

In the New Testament, God revealed himself to Paul in a vision. "Now as he went on his way, he approached Damascus, and suddenly a light from heaven shone around him. And falling to the ground, he heard a voice saying to him, "Saul, Saul, why are you persecuting me?" And he said, "Who are you, Lord?" And he said, "I am Jesus, whom you are persecuting'" (Acts 9:3–5). God also spoke to both Cornelius and Peter through visions (Acts 10:3–6, 10–16). These visions resulted in the gospel being preached to the gentiles for the very first time! In fact, all of us who are non-Jews today can call ourselves believers because of these encounters. Finally, we know about God's plans for the end times because of his encounters through visions with the apostle John on the island of Patmos: "I was in the Spirit on the Lord's day, and I heard behind me a loud voice like a trumpet saying, 'Write what you see in a book and send it to the seven churches, to Ephesus and to Smyrna and to Pergamum and to Thyatira and to Sardis and to Philadelphia and to Laodicea'" (Rev. 1:10–11).

The Greek word for "vision" in the New Testament is *horama*. It refers to visions that we have in the night, to experiences that we have in our sleep, and to visions that we have while we are awake. "When Moses saw it, he was amazed at the sight, and as he drew near to look, there came the voice of the Lord: 'I am the God of your fathers, the God of Abraham and of Isaac and of Jacob.' And Moses trembled and did not dare to look" (Acts 7:31–32). A common Greek word for "dream" in the New Testament is *onar* which means a vision that we have while sleeping. "But as he considered these things, behold, an angel of the Lord appeared to him in a dream, saying, 'Joseph, son of David, do not fear to take Mary as your wife, for that which is conceived in her is from the Holy Spirit'" (Matt. 1:20). Finally, the Greek word *ekstasis* is often translated as the word "trance" in the New Testament. It means to stand aside from yourself and can refer to experiences that you have when you're awake or asleep. "The next day, as they were on their journey and approaching the city, Peter went up on the housetop about the sixth hour to pray. And he became hungry and wanted something to eat, but while they were preparing it, he fell into a trance" (Acts 10:9–10).

Most of the visions that I have had have been while prophesying over other people. They have been "closed visions," or visions in which I was a spectator looking at what was happening. Sometimes, however, God gives us "open visions." An open vision is one in which we are no longer spectators, but active participants in the experience. Dick and I were on a camping vacation and during the night I woke up and found myself sitting at a table in a café on a bright sunny day. The person sitting across from me was someone who I had not had any contact with for several years. In fact, our last conversation had been very unpleasant. He looked at me and said, "Arleen, I'm really glad that you're here. I've been praying and asking God to give me the chance to speak to you. I didn't have your address and I want to apologize for the way I behaved the last time we met. Will you please forgive me?" Hearing him say those words brought me a lot of comfort, and of course I forgave him. He told me about his life and all that had happened to him since we last saw each other. Several times during the experience I pinched myself to see if I was awake. It felt so real! I reached out to touch his hand just to make sure he was real. And sure enough, he was! The next morning I got up wondering what had happened the night before. I know that I was not asleep. I had the bruises on my hand from where I kept pinching myself to prove it! This vision helped me deal with the situation and brought emotional healing, when I had no other way of contacting him.

Different Types of Dreams

Prophetic dreams bring comfort, give warnings, proclaim events and can open the door to deep emotional healing.

DREAMS RELATED TO EMOTIONAL HEALING

God regularly uses dreams in my life. On one occasion, I had a powerful dream. You'll need to know a bit of backstory for this. Soon after Dick and I planted our church, God's Embassy, it was discovered that the Senior Pastor of the previous church that we had been in had fallen into sin. He was also the leader of our denomination. Eventually the church and the denomination fell apart and many people ended up hurt and disillusioned. It was around this time that I had the first of two dreams related to what had happened. In the dream I drove my car into the parking lot of a church I'd never been to before. I was there to attend a conference. As I walked into the building, someone I didn't know called my name. They came running over to me. They said, "You're late and you've got to do the announcements!" They then shoved a microphone into my hand and told me that the meeting was about to start and that I should hurry to the auditorium. I frantically ran through the building trying to find someone who could tell me what the announcements were that I needed to make. I even went up to the sound booth, which was accessed by a flight of stairs, to ask. No one knew. I still remember the deep sense of frustration I felt as I took my seat at the front of the auditorium not knowing what I was supposed to say and not knowing that I was a part of the organizing committee until I had gotten there! When it was time for me to go up on stage I just stood there looking at the audience not knowing what to say. That's when I woke up.

One of the ways that I know that a dream is from God is because of the intensity of the emotion accompanying the dream. My husband tells me that I sometimes weep in my sleep because of a dream. He has also heard me praying in tongues loudly while dreaming, in addition to commanding demons to be bound and to leave. Dreams that originate from our souls are different from God dreams. They are usually not as intense and the themes and storylines seem to go in all sorts of different directions.

Sometimes God won't show us the meaning of our dreams and visions immediately. Instead, He will ask us to persevere in prayer until He gives us the meaning. I wrote down the dream in my journal (spiritual diary) and prayed about it because it had felt so real. I didn't know what it meant until two years later, when I went to a church whose building I'd never been in before to attend a prophetic conference. I was part of the team that had organized the conference and the other organizers asked me if I would open the conference and do the announcements. I did and then sat back down. During a break I went up to the sound booth to get some peace and quiet. The floor was carpeted and I lay down in a corner. I rested there with my eyes closed enjoying the sounds of the worship team as they played a few numbers in preparation for the next session. When I eventually opened my eyes and looked around it dawned on me that I had seen this place before, even though I knew that I had never been in this building. All of a sudden it hit me. This was the building that I had been in in my dream! Everything looked exactly the same. But this time I wasn't speechless. I was a legitimate part of the leadership of the conference and was able to speak and have my voice be heard. I started to cry.

All that time I had been unable to talk freely about what had happened regarding our former Senior Pastor. I was disappointed and indignant. I had been shocked and hurt, but the topic was confidential. It was so sensitive that I was unable to talk about it to the people around me. I was told, "You should forgive and move on with your life." Though that is true, it is also important to communicate your feelings. This dream made me realize I was allowed to speak about this, that it was important for me to talk about it. Afterwards, I was able to share how I felt with someone trustworthy. These talks brought deep healing and also made me aware of a root dating back to my childhood, which I subsequently dealt with.

WARNING DREAMS

God can speak to us to warn us through dreams. He does this to both believers and non-believers. "But God came to Abimelech in a dream by night and said to him, 'Behold, you are a dead man because of the woman you have taken, for she is a man's wife'" (Gen. 20:3). "While he was sitting on the judgment seat, his wife sent word to him, "Have nothing to do with that righteous man, for I have suffered much because of him today in a dream'" (Matt. 27:19). Both Abimelech and Pilate's wife had nightmares. The distinguishing feature of a nightmare is that the dreamer is in danger.[13] Sometimes God will use a dream that startles or frightens us to get our attention, as in the case of Abimelech. Through the nightmare God let him know that Sarah was married to someone else. He gave Sarah back to Abraham and God spared his life. Not all dreams are from God: nightmares can be ways for tormenting demonic spirits to harass us and to rob us of our peace and joy. This seems to have happened to Pilate's wife.

When I teach dream interpretation classes, people often come up to me and say that they've had dreams in the past about people having accidents or something happening to them and they don't know what to do. They're usually flustered because the dreams are so real! I tell them that these things are not just premonitions, but that this is God letting them know that it's time to get up and to pray that what they're seeing doesn't happen.

In her book *Dreams and Visions*,[14] respected prophet Jane Hamon describes having a vivid dream about her brother one night. In the dream she saw her brother having a serious accident and dying. She woke up shocked and took action: she started to pray that God would protect his life. The next morning her mother called and said, "I just wanted to let you know that your brother crashed his car into a tree last night. The car was a total wreck, but your brother got out safely!" In another dream she saw the same brother getting very ill and dying. Once again, she got up and prayed. A while later she was talking to her mother. At the end of the conversation her mother said, "Your brother's appendix burst and he had to be rushed to hospital for emergency surgery. It was quite serious and he almost died. You don't have to worry though. The operation went well and the doctor says that your brother will be fine." It was obvious that Jane's brother needed lots of protection at that time in his life and because of Jane's relationship with God, she knew what to do when He gave her these dreams.

PEOPLE SPEAKING TO YOU IN DREAMS

Have you ever dreamt that specific people speak to you? I regularly meet people who tell me that I came to them in a dream and told them things. When they say this, my response is always, "When you see people in your dreams, you need to ask yourself what that person symbolizes to you. It could be that I represent someone who is a trusted prophetic voice. I didn't come to you personally in your dream because I was in my own bed sleeping at the time!" I then ask them what they were told.

I myself have also experienced this phenomenon. Years ago I had a dream in which Stacey Campbell was talking to me. She told me that God would open doors for me to travel to different nations by January 1st. I knew it wasn't Stacey who had come to me in person, but that she represented a trusted prophetic voice in my life. I therefore paid close attention to the dream. I also knew that January 1st didn't necessarily mean January 1st of the next year, but that it meant the beginning of the new phase that I was entering. When I did get my first invitation to travel a few years later I was able to accept it freely because God has already spoken to me about it. These days I regularly travel abroad to minister.

Interpreting Dreams

God is the Giver of dreams. He will often give us dreams to show us the state of our own hearts, to open our ears and to bypass pride in our lives (Gen. 20:3; Dan. 2:30; Job 33:16–17). He also gives us dreams to show us what's going to happen, to warn us and to guide us (for biblical examples of this, see Matt. 1–2). However, not all dreams are from God. The devil can send tormenting or deceptive dreams. He comes "only to steal and kill and destroy" (John 10:10). In order to test the provenance of a dream, we could assess its fruit. If it is negative, and the dream only frightens us and does not bring peace, it does not come from God.

Therefore, the first step in dream interpretation is to pray and to ask God whether or not the dream is from Him and if so, for His help in interpreting it. The second step is to write down your dream in as much detail as possible. It is handy to make sure that you have a writing pad beside your bed at night. Taking notes on your mobile phone is also good. The third step is to make a list of the symbols in the dream. Step four is to write down the meaning of the dream as God gives it to you. Obviously, the interpretation will need to agree with the heart of God as found in the Bible. If the dream indicates a change of direction in your life, talk to your spiritual advisors before acting (Chapter 6). Finally, if the Lord is using the dream to give a warning, pray about it and seek wisdom from someone you can trust.

As we continue with the topic of dream interpretation, I want to talk a bit more about step three—make a list of the symbols in the dream. The vast majority of our dreams are symbolic rather than literal. This is very important to understand if we're going to be able to interpret dreams. Since God is the Giver of dreams, He is also the One who gives the interpretation. Therefore, to be able to interpret dreams correctly we must know the language of signs and symbols, but more importantly, we must know God (Gen. 41:16; Dan. 2:27–28). Some common symbols are:

HOUSES AND BUILDINGS – The Bible compares our lives to a house: The wise man builds his house (his life) upon the rock (Matt. 7:24–27). The rule of thumb is that if a dream takes place in a home that you're living in now, then God is trying to tell you something about yourself through the dream that's relevant to you now. If a dream takes place in a home that you lived in in the past, then He's often trying to tell you something about your past.

VEHICLES – Are there any vehicles or other forms of transport in the dream? For example, are you sitting in a car and if so, where? Are you the one doing the driving (responsibility/control), or are you sitting in the passenger seat or in the back? How do you feel about where you are sitting? It could be that God is challenging you to change seats, take responsibility and to get behind the wheel. If you're travelling in a bus, it could be that you're going along with the crowd.

ANIMALS – With animals it's always important to ask yourself the question, "What does this animal mean to me? What does it evoke?" For example, a barking dog can be a friendly image for those who love dogs, but very threatening to people who are afraid of them.

NUMBERS – There are some commonly accepted interpretations of numbers. One: unity, God. Two: agreement. Three: the Trinity. Four: the earth (the four corners of the earth). Five: grace, salvation, the fivefold ministry. Six: the number of man. Seven: completion. Eight: new beginnings. Nine: manifestation of the Spirit. Ten: judgment. Eleven: grace. Twelve: the reign of God, government. Thirteen: double blessing, double cursing.

COLORS – Which colors are prominent in your dreams? In colors, too, there are commonly accepted interpretations. Red: the blood of Christ/passion. White: purity. Green: life. Yellow: joy or cowardice. Gold: glory. Blue: God, hope, healing, depression. Purple: regal, kingdom.

There are many good reference materials on symbols available on the internet. However, always ask the Lord what that symbol means in the context of this particular dream.

Take Your Time

Sometimes we will need to be patient. God may not respond immediately, but may want us to persevere in prayer with Him for the deeper meaning of the dream and a deeper understanding of who He is. A few months ago I had a dream that made such an impression on me that I when I woke up I was very disturbed. This feeling was accentuated by my husband asking me what I'd been dreaming about the night before; he said that he'd heard me crying in my sleep.

In my dream I was in the Youth With A Mission building here in Amsterdam. I've been there often to teach at their Discipleship Training Schools (DTS) and in the dream I was rushing to an office that I had in the building during a break in one my DTS teaching sessions. I rushed in and found the papers that I needed on my desk. As I turned to go back to the classroom, I noticed something white lying on the ground. It was flat like a piece of paper. I picked it up and realized with horror that it was my white terrier dog. I always kept my office locked and he had died from neglect because I'd been too busy even to give him water. He was completely dehydrated. Suddenly, I saw his mouth move just a tiny little bit. I shouted for someone to bring me water and while I held the dog's mouth open, they dribbled a few drops of water into his mouth. His heartbeat was so weak that I thought that he would die. I was devastated. I loved this dog and kept asking myself as I wept, how could I have ever forgotten him? I still remember the feeling of deep remorse. We prayed for him and carefully laid him down in a blanket on one of the chairs in the room. With a heavy heart I returned to my classroom. A few hours later when the lesson was over, I went back to my office dreading the thought of finding the dog now dead. I had hardly finished opening the office door when something white and fuzzy jumped into my arms and started licking my face. I couldn't believe it. The dog was alive and well! I fell to my knees crying and thanking the Lord that He had spared the dog's life, vowing to never let that happen again. From that moment on, caring for the dog that God had given back to me would be my highest priority.

The emotions that came with that dream were so intense that I knew that this had to be a dream from God. I started to pray and write down the details of the dream. I really needed to know what God was trying to say to me. In the end it took more than five months before He gave me the interpretation. But I kept going back to God on it because I knew that it was important. The fact that the dream had taken place in the YWAM building told me that the Lord was saying something about my ministry life. The fact that I was running to my office and that things were rushed was clear enough. The thing that really stumped me for a long time was the dog. I don't actually own a dog. I like dogs and I think that terriers are particularly friendly. My strong emotional reaction to the dog's death told me that the dog represented something that was very precious to me. The fact that he was white told me that he had something to do with purity.

Months later, when I was in the middle of doing something completely unrelated to the dream it suddenly hit me what the dog was. It represented my relationship with the Lord. I stopped what I was doing and sat down. God had been trying to tell me through that dream that I had become too busy, and as a result had neglected my relationship with Him. I was still praying and having my times alone with Him, but He really wanted me to spend extended time walking and talking with Him. I also realized that that was why I was so upset. This dream had everything to do with my relationship with Him and a level of communion that both He and I were missing.

CHAPTER 5

Prophetic Protocol

Protocol is the wisdom element in the prophetic and, as such, it is important. It means that in every situation, time or place, there is a correct way to handle things.

"My pastor is against the Holy Spirit!" This was the frustrated cry of a lady in one of our Schools of the Prophets one day. I knew her pastor and I knew that while he was cautious about the gifts of the Spirit, he wasn't "against the Holy Spirit." I asked her to tell me what had happened. She said, "Yesterday during worship in our church service the pastor said that if anyone had a word from God they could come on stage and deliver it to the church. I had a word, so I went up and said it. Last night he called me at home and he was mad. He told me that I wasn't allowed to prophesy in church anymore."

I asked her, "What did you say?"

She said, "God said that the Holy Spirit wasn't honored there and that if the church leaders didn't repent, He would remove His Spirit from the church completely!"

I looked at her and said, "I can understand why your pastor was upset. He's not against the Holy Spirit. You just didn't use the proper protocol." I then went on to explain to her how she could have handled things.

Months later, she told me that after our talk she'd gone back and apologized to her pastor for how she shared the word. During the year that she was with us being trained, both he and I saw her change. She is prophetic, but she also learned to act with wisdom. Years later she is now the leader of the prophetic ministry teams in the same church.

Protocol, defined as a code of diplomatic or military etiquette, is important. In medicine it is defined as "the right way to do things." In the prophetic it means that in every situation, time or place, there is a correct way to handle things. For years prophets around the world have been prophesying that God is raising the level of prophetic revelation and authority. They say that we will stand before presidents and kings with the prophetic word of the Lord. I am convinced that this word applies to many of God's prophetic people and not just a handful of those especially gifted in the prophetic. But if I'm honest, I have only seen a handful of people who fit that brief. One of the main reasons for this is that many of us don't know how to act when we prophesy. Without knowing the protocol behind delivering prophetic words we run the risk of not being heard when we have a true word from the Lord, or worse yet, not even getting to speak to the person for whom the word is meant.

Unfortunately, I have met prophetic people who, if I hadn't known better, would have tempted me to close the doors of our church to the prophetic. In our desire to be open to the work of the Holy Spirit and to allow maximum freedom for those who want to step out in using their spiritual gifts, we have neglected to teach people how to behave. In the book of Ephesians, Paul talks about the "Spirit of wisdom and revelation" (Eph. 1:17). I find it very noteworthy that he mentions wisdom before revelation. Prophetic words may well fall flat if they are given without using wisdom. And I have to admit that I myself have made mistakes in this area. These are some of the things I've learned and consequently teach.

Basic Protocol

When prophesying over people, first of all, it's best to speak clearly and use normal everyday words that people, even those who don't believe, can understand. In our Schools of the Prophets we are not just training people to prophesy in churches, but also into every single sphere of influence in society. This means that we need to be clear enough when we prophesy that the person for whom the word is meant can act on the word once they've tested it. For example, say someone prophesies, "I see that the Lord is going to open up new doors of opportunity to you. Doors that weren't open before." You might think that this word is encouraging. It's certainly meant to be. It would be helpful, however, if the person over whom you're prophesying knew a bit more about which doors God is going to open and in what area. Is it work? Is it ministry? Is it relationships? It helps them to know which direction to look in so that they can better recognize when the word has been fulfilled.

One of the words used to describe prophecy in the Bible is the word *nabi*. It means "to bubble up" and describes what happens when we open our mouths and begin prophesying. Often much more comes out than we bargained for. Many of us have been trained to say only what we feel that we've received at that moment. I often hear people say in our schools, "Yes, but that's all I've got." I really believe that God is a good God and that He *wants* us to know His will. If God gave the initial revelation, He will give more if we learn to ask Him for more revelation and wait for it in faith. He always does.

It is also almost always better to be short and concise when prophesying. One afternoon Dick and I went to receive prophetic ministry at a conference we were attending. People could sign up to receive a prophetic word from a member of the ministry team, so we did. The person ministering to us was a dear lady. As she started to speak I could feel the anointing behind her words. She prophesied over us for about ten minutes. When she was done I looked at Dick and said, "Did you feel the anointing on that word? It was wonderful!"

Dick, however, looked at me and said, "Yes, but she didn't say anything!" We'd recorded her prophetic word and when I got home and typed it out, I discovered that what she did say could have been said in two sentences without losing any of the anointing. In the prophetic, longer is not always better!

In our activations we regularly use time limits on how long people can prophesy, for example thirty seconds, to teach them how to get to the point. Interestingly enough, the people who have the most problems with this in the beginning are those who have had the most experience with prophecy in the past. It's because they've never done it this way before. The training probably sounds quite spartan, but we offer our students a safe environment so that they are not afraid to prophesy when they go out into the world. We have a lot of fun together too and people tend to make friends for life by the time we're done.

Another important point in protocol is that it is important to turn a negative into a positive. God's character in us is more important than our gifts. As we prophesy over people in love, they will want to get to know the One who is the source of the prophetic words. But being loving doesn't mean that we close our eyes to character flaws that God wants to highlight. The challenge is to turn the negative thing God is letting us see into something that invites the receiver to come closer to God, so that He can meet them and deal with it.

For example, suppose you are praying for someone and the Lord shows you that there is sexual impurity in that person's life. You could say, "God shows me that there is sexual impurity in your life and you need to repent of this sinful behavior now!" The word may be true, but presenting it like that would make them cautious about approaching God, especially if you're prophesying over them in a group. It creates insecurity: God must have sent someone to call out their sins like that in public! But that's not true and it's not according to His character.

When You're Wrong

It doesn't matter how gifted we are in the prophetic, sometimes we will deliver an inaccurate prophetic word. In the Bible, Paul says that our prophesying (here on earth) is "incomplete" (1 Cor. 13:9). This means that we will sometimes make mistakes. When we do it's important to say sorry, especially if we end up hurting someone with our words.

Once I was prophesying over the leaders of a local church in Amsterdam while speaking at a conference they had organized. The church leaders had asked me to prophesy over their staff members. When I got to one of the assistant pastors, I looked at her. The sensation of fruitfulness coming from her was almost overwhelming. I also saw a baby. I know that babies usually refer to new ministries that someone is about to give birth to, but this was far too strong to only be figurative, or so I thought. I prophesied that I saw great fruitfulness all over her and this would be both in the spiritual and natural. As I did, she fell to the ground. God encountered her deeply that day. After the meeting ended, she came to me and told me that the prophetic word had really encouraged her. She and her husband had been trying to have children for years without success. This had given her hope that one day they would have children after all. After listening to her even I was encouraged.

But about a year later I got a phone call. It was someone from that same church. The person called to tell me that this lady was scheduled to have major surgery to remove her womb. She had been diagnosed with uterine cancer. I was devastated. Her church and many others had been praying for her for weeks but to no avail. She hadn't been healed and would have to have the operation.

After she had recovered enough to return to work, I called and asked her if I could come by. I told her that I didn't know why things had gone so drastically wrong and asked her to forgive me for raising her expectations and hope that some-day God would give her her own biological child. That was now obviously totally impossible. She told me that she appreciated the fact that I came along to apologize. To this day I still don't know how I could have missed it so badly.

Your Own Attitude

It should always be our intention to bless people with our prophesying. It is not about us or our egos, so we should not get offended when they do not accept our words. This is one of those lessons that I had to learn the hard way. One day I was praying for people who had come to receive prayer after a church service. I looked at a lady and saw a huge and very real spirit of death over her life. I was shocked and confused. I knew her and she was the picture of health. As far as I knew she was not sick.

I prayed for her and commanded the spirit of death to leave her immediately! As I did, she fell to the ground. I then proceeded to speak the life of Christ over her as well as the perfect health that Christ had died to give her. She lay on the ground for forty-five minutes before getting up and going home. The next week she came and spoke to me. She said, "You remember what you prayed for me last week? You prayed about a spirit of death and commanded it to leave me. Well, it does not resonate with me at all. So I'm here to let you know that I reject what you saw. I also reject that whole falling in the Spirit thing. I don't think that it's from God." I looked at her in total disbelief! I kept thinking about how God had met her that day and it was as if we were talking about two completely different events. I was also offended that someone would reject what I considered to be the work of God in their life like she had just done. In the end I said "okay" and let her go. That moment I also made a decision that I would live to regret. I decided that I was not going to pray for her. If she was going to reject such a powerful encounter from God like that, then I wasn't going to pray. Even as I write these words, I see myself standing with my arms crossed. I now realize that I looked more like a four-year-old who hadn't gotten her own way than an "anointed prophet of God."

A while later I got a telephone call. The person who phoned told me that this lady was in the hospital fighting for her life. She had been diagnosed with non-Hodgkin lymphoma and was having to undergo some intensive rounds of chemo-therapy. Things were not going well and her husband had asked this person to call me and to ask me to pray. When I hung up the phone, I felt like someone had just kicked me in the stomach, and I started to cry. I knew that the spirit of death was after her. I had allowed myself to become offended when she rejected the word and I had hardened my heart by deciding not to pray for her. I cried for hours and repented of my bad attitude. I also pleaded with God to save her life. God answered that prayer, but in total she needed at least six rounds of chemotherapy before the doctors finally said that she was healed. That sickness dominated her life, and the lives of her family members, for years.

I determined for myself that I would never again allow myself to become offended when people do not receive the prophetic words I give them. I will also continue to pray for them when I know that the enemy is pursuing them. After all, the prophetic words that we receive for people are from God and not from ourselves. We just have to do the best we can to bring the word. How people receive it is a matter between them and God, and that is where we need to leave the words after we have spoken them out—with God.

Protocol for Leaders

People are often surprised when I say there is a protocol around prophesying over leaders. I don't just mean church leaders, but all leaders. Their thinking is that "leaders are people too, so why should you treat them differently from anyone else?" One of the main reasons is because of the level of responsibility that leaders carry.

Meeting government leaders will often have a different protocol than meeting other types of leaders. If you don't know the right protocol and stick to it, you might find yourself being ushered out of the meeting very quickly. It's also very important you stick to the amount of time allotted for your meeting. I recently had the honor of being part of a small group that met with the sitting president of a South American nation. His aide, who was a friend of one of the members of our group, told us that even if we were in the middle of an interesting conversation, when it was time to go we should stop, say goodbye and leave. He told us that the president was always very polite, but that those who stayed longer than the time they had been given were never invited back. In these kinds of situations it is important to get to the point.

Similar protocols apply when prophesying in a church. If you have been invited to prophesy in a service or during a conference, make sure that you know what the protocol is before you start. Ask yourself how familiar the people you're ministering to are with the prophetic and whether they are used to people speaking out prophetic words from the front. I am constantly surprised by the number of leaders who tell me that nobody has ever asked them those questions before. Where churches are less familiar with the prophetic, we should discuss before the service how they would like us to deliver the prophetic words. Honoring their protocol can lead to the door being opened for the prophetic in a congregation or group. It is important to say here that if God does give you a word of correction for people, or for the leadership, these should always be shared privately. As I mentioned before, it is important to share prophetic words in a loving way.

There are occasions when prophecy should be given to leaders privately and not in a group setting. For example, when prophetic words might indicate a change of leadership. In 1 Kings 11, Jeroboam received a prophetic word from the prophet Ahijah telling him that God was going to tear ten of the tribes of Israel away from Solomon because of Solomon's great sin of worshiping other gods. The tribes would be given to Jeroboam. Solomon found out about this and tried to kill Jeroboam. He didn't succeed. Later, after Solomon's death, this prophecy was fulfilled.

In 2 Kings 9:1–3 the prophet Elisha called one of the members of his prophetic group to him. He gave him a flask of oil and told him to go find Jehu. When he did, he was supposed to pour the oil over Jehu's head and anoint him to be king over Israel. I love what it says at the end of verse 3, "Then open the door and run for your life!" (NLT) Being a prophet in Old Testament times was never boring. The member of Elijah's prophetic group did as he was told. Later, Jehu destroyed Ahab and Jezebel's entire dynasty.

I am invited regularly to pray for the leadership teams of churches. Sometimes God shows me that He is preparing one of the younger members of the team to become the senior leader. This usually goes hand in hand with a word for the senior leader that says that God is preparing them for a role in which they start to minister more regularly outside the local church. When this happens, I never prophesy this in the group or in public. I usually call the senior and junior leader aside and prophesy this word to them in private. I also make sure that I explain that one of the most difficult things to determine in prophecy is timing. God may be preparing the younger leader for more responsibility in leadership but it might take several years before the word is fulfilled. In these situations, I encourage the senior leader to start to think about ways that they can start to prepare the younger leader for a greater level of responsibility in leadership.

Last year I was asked to prophesy over a group from the US and the senior leader was not able to travel with them. In that situation I had the junior leader record the word and told him to let the senior leader listen to it and test it. I also told the junior leader that he had to wait on God's timing to be elevated and not to take things into his own hands.

Words of Correction

Most of the time when God lets us see negative things in people's lives it is so that we can pray for them. This is true especially if we don't know them that well. We need to pray that they allow God to touch them in these areas so that they can bring them into the light and deal with them. But sometimes God continues to talk to us about these things and He asks us to speak to the people concerned about what He is showing us. This is one of the greatest challenges a prophetic person faces. Samuel's example of how he dealt with King Saul is a model for us to follow if God should ever call us to speak out a word of correction.

Many years earlier, Samuel had ordained Saul to be Israel's first king. Character issues, especially Saul's refusal to obey

God completely (1 Sam. 15:1-9), had been a recurring theme in Saul's reign. Finally, God said to Samuel, "I regret that I have made Saul king, for he has turned back from following me and has not performed my commandments" (1 Sam. 15:11). Samuel was so deeply moved when he heard this that he cried out to God all night before going to see Saul the next day. In our Schools of the Prophets I teach that you're ready to correct someone after you have fasted and prayed for them long enough that you can see them through God's eyes. At that point, you would almost rather have the negative effects of their sin fall on you than on them. Only after we have allowed God to break our hearts for those in sin can we speak to them effectively.

A highly respected and internationally recognized prophetic leader told me that God had spoken to her several times in a dream about the sins of a leader of a large denomination. After she had prayed, she and her husband went to talk to this man in private. Instead of acknowledging that God was trying to talk to him and give him a chance to repent, the leader denied everything. He was very upset and after the meeting he made her life extremely difficult by trying to damage her reputation whenever he got the chance. This continued for four years before his sins became front page news. I spoke to the prophetic leader about this and asked her how she had been able to deal with the pressure of the whole situation. I will never forget her words. "Arleen, as a prophet you have to obey God no matter what the consequences are for yourself or for your ministry."

Protocol for Churches

I encourage church leaders who want to develop a healthy prophetic ministry within their churches to sit down with their leadership teams and to develop their own prophetic protocol. Prophecy can be an immense blessing, but it functions best when there is a clear protocol in place that is known and understood by all of the members. Different churches will have different protocols depending on their vision and mission.

God's Embassy has its own prophetic protocol, and it works. I was surprised when a national intercessory prayer leader in the Netherlands told me, "Arleen, don't you know that your church is considered to be the prophetic church in the nation? You're the ones we point to when we talk about how to be healthy in the prophetic." Our church is part of a larger apostolic center Dick and I have established. I would therefore not have been surprised if she had said "apostolic." However, we are a church in which prophecy is considered to be normal and in which apostles and prophets work together in a healthy way. I'll say more about this in a later chapter.

Since prophecy is a normal part of who we are, we want everyone to know how to hear God's voice for themselves and to prophesy. This has a few practical consequences. First, twice a year, usually on the first Sunday in January and the first Sunday in September, everyone can come to receive prophetic ministry from our prophetic teams after the service. The teams prophesy destiny words (words about people's gifts and callings) over everyone from the youngest babies to the oldest senior citizens. Everyone is encouraged to record the words spoken out during these times and to pray into them during the coming season. Not surprisingly, these are some of our best-attended services.

Since apostles, prophets, evangelists, pastors and teachers are called to equip people to do God's work in whatever sphere of society they are called to (Eph. 4: 11–13), we use these times of prophecy to whet people's appetites to hear the voice of God for themselves and we encourage them to be trained in our Schools of the Prophets. We teach them to test the words and then to act on those words that have passed the testing process.

People regularly have prophetic impressions during our services. When they do, they can come forward and share their impressions with the member of our team who is leading the service that day. The team member is the one who decides whether the word is relevant or applicable to what they feel the Holy Spirit is doing during the service. Speakers are free to prophesy. We do, however, let them know beforehand that we are a church that tests revelation. After we have done this, we try to get back to them to let them know what we feel that the Lord has confirmed.

Our Code of Conduct

A few years ago we set up a code of conduct for prophets and prophetic ministers that we now teach in our Schools of the Prophets (Appendix). This has been very helpful in establishing a healthy prophetic culture in our church, and in the churches our students call home and nationally. I encourage you to read it and find an accountability partner to help you to apply this in your own life. If you're a pastor, I would like to encourage you to discuss these statements with your leadership team and determine which are relevant for your own situation.

Testing Prophetic Revelation

The Bible says to "test everything; hold fast what is good" (1 Thess. 5:21). For most of us this testing process consists solely of us having an agreement in our spirits. While this is one way to test prophetic revelation, it is often the most subjective.

A while ago I was at a revival meeting. The speaker was a well-known revivalist evangelist and the Holy Spirit was present with power. As the meeting was coming to an end, the speaker asked the 1,400 people present to come forward if they wanted to know the will of God for their lives but didn't. I was standing at the side of the room enjoying what was going on when I heard the Lord say to me, "I want you to watch what happens now." Somewhat surprised, I stood and began to pay attention to who was responding to the altar call.

I have been around in charismatic circles in the Netherlands for years and I knew many of the people who were coming forward for prayer. I'd also been in meetings before where many of these same people had been prayed for for the same thing by different prophetic ministers. As the Lord brought back to my mind their callings, I started to get uncomfortable. I thought, "How can they say that they don't know what their calling is?" Now I was really disturbed.

After the ministry time I went forward and talked to some of them. I asked them about the previous words that they had received and why they had gone up for ministry again this time. One by one they told me the same story.

Yes, they had received prophetic words in the past about their callings. In fact, many of these words lined up with the words they'd just gotten. They knew the call of God on their lives, but they hadn't yet seen the words fulfilled. My heart ached for them when some of them told me that they had been waiting for 14 years!

As I dug deeper, I learned that many of them had no idea what to do with a prophetic word after being prophesied over by someone. They had been taught that if a prophetic word was from God then He would fulfill it without any help from them. They said, "God doesn't need our help." I call this the "casino slot machine" approach to the prophetic. The thinking is that if you receive enough words, something just might happen one day. In fact, doing anything at all, they thought, would be the same as trying to make something happen in your own strength. Actually, the opposite is true. Not doing anything is a sure recipe for disappointment. It's also not biblical. God is at work restoring the authority of the prophetic ministry by demonstrating without question that prophecy works. When He speaks through prophecy we can and should expect things to happen.

The Bible says to "test everything; hold fast what is good" (1 Thess. 5:21). For most of us, including many who have prophesied for years and who are very experienced in the prophetic, this testing process consists solely of us having a "click" in our spirit about a word. In other words, our spirit resonates with the word that was given. While this is one way to test prophetic revelation, it is often the most subjective way. It is also not enough when you need to make important decisions that are going to affect the course of your family, work, or ministry based on prophetic revelation.

How to Test

The first thing to do with a prophetic word is to record it. We should then write it down (like the Lord told Habakkuk to do, Hab. 2:2). Everyone who knows me knows that I think that the smartphone is an invention from heaven! Because of it, almost all of us have a mobile recording device with us at all times. Even though we think that we will remember a powerful prophetic word, we usually don't. The words are often too long to remember and we can get emotional when our spirits recognize God's voice in a prophetic word. Writing down the word after we've recorded it helps us to see things that we didn't see when the word was originally spoken. I can't count the number of times when writing out a word that I wound up thinking, "I thought that this meant that, but I see now that what I thought I'd heard is different from what was actually said!" This is really important, because we all have a tendency to hear what we want to hear.

I once prophesied over a lady who was a single mom. She had three young daughters and her husband was in jail for domestic violence. She was discouraged and was having a hard time. As I prophesied over her, I saw her in a business suit walking through the halls of 10 Downing Street. That's the address of the British Prime Minister. When I was done, she said, "That's a great word, but did God show you my future husband?" I said no, but I also let her know that no single prophetic word will show you God's entire will for your life. Abraham, for example, received twelve different prophetic words from God during his lifetime. God was speaking to me about her job, but that did not mean that He did not have a husband for her in the future somewhere.

It was an encouraging word . . . or so I thought. A few hours later I heard from someone that this lady was in her room weeping uncontrollably because I had prophesied that she was never going to get married. When she'd calmed down, I spoke to her and asked her to replay what I'd said. I also made sure that there were others present as witnesses. After she listened again, she brightened up. She looked up at me and said, "I really thought that you said that I'd never get married, but you didn't." A short time later, this lady got a new job and nine months after that she emailed me to let me know that she'd been at 10 Downing Street, at the office of the British Prime Minister the week before on a consulting job for her work. She said, "I wouldn't have had the courage to say yes to this if it hadn't been for that prophetic word that you gave me." The last sentence of her email really made me smile. "By the way, has God said anything yet about my future husband?"

After we've recorded and written down the word, the next thing to do is to pray and ask God to speak to us about the word as we test it. If the word is simply encouraging, comforting or meant to build us up, for example that "God sees you and will be with you," we just need to say thank you and amen. I call these words "inspirational words." Since they are based on the truth of the Bible and since they don't require to us to do anything that could be life-changing or have serious consequences, you usually don't have to test them very rigorously.

Words of direction, correction and destiny (our gifts and callings) do need to be tested for both the content and the timing. Timing is extremely tricky in the prophetic and it's the most difficult thing to get right. Since God is eternal, for Him a thousand years is like a day. For us however, a thousand years is a very long time. In my experience, when God says "immediately" it usually means some time in the next two or three years. When God says "soon" that could mean anything from four to ten years. If God says "not now, but later" then you know you're in for a long wait.

An important thing to determine with any directional, correctional or destiny word is what kind of spirit is at the root of it. Jesus said that a good tree cannot produce bad fruit and a bad tree cannot produce good fruit (Matt. 7:17). Words from the Holy Spirit produce the fruit of the Spirit in our lives—"love, joy, peace, patience, kindness, goodness, faithfulness, gentleness [and] self-control" (Gal. 5:22–23). If any other type of fruit is produced, you need to seriously question the source of the prophetic word. The words can sound very spiritual and still have a demonic spirit as their source. The slave girl from Philippi who had a spirit that enabled her to tell the future said about Paul and his friends, "These men are servants of the Most High God, and they have come to tell you how to be saved" (Acts 16:17, NLT). The words she spoke were correct, but the spirit behind them was not!

Demonically Inspired Words

During the lunch break at one of our Schools of the Prophets, I spoke to a man who was really struggling. He and his wife were church leaders and five years earlier they had invited a prophet in their denomination to come and speak at their church. Someone they knew had recommended him. During the service this prophet had a word for him and his wife. He said, "Son, the Lord says that it is going to get very stormy for you and your family in the next few years. I see that the Lord is going to test you like he tested Job. If you hold onto your faith, however, you will prevail." The word sounded theologically sound, even to my ears. He then went on to tell me that since then his oldest son had had a motorcycle accident and was now paralyzed from the waist down. His youngest son saw what happened to his brother and blamed God for all that had happened. He and his wife had also been constantly in and out of the hospital with different illnesses during that time. He said, "Is this really God? I don't know what to do anymore."

He was obviously in distress. As I quietly prayed and waited on the Lord, all of a sudden I knew what the problem was—the spirit behind the word was not from God! When I told him this he looked confused. I said, "It's really quite simple. Jesus said a good tree cannot produce bad fruit, but fruit in line with the Holy Spirit. The devil is out to 'steal and kill and destroy' (John 10:10). Would you say that the fruit of that prophetic word was good?"

He looked at me and said, "No, not at all."

I continued, "It seems to me that what you and your family are experiencing is more in line with the work of the enemy (stealing, killing and destroying) than with the Holy Spirit."

He said, "But isn't this just a fulfillment of the prophetic word?"

"We'll find out," I responded.

I then suggested that we pray out loud and break the power of those words over this man and his family, since that particular word seemed to be working as a curse on their lives. It is important to do this in these kinds of situations. The Bible teaches that we bless and curse people by our words (Prov. 18:21; Ps. 10:7; Ps. 118:26). If we want to break the power of a prophetic word that we do not recognize as being from God after we've tested it, we need to do it out loud. We just need to pray, "I do not accept this word and I break its power over my life in Jesus' name!" We did this, and afterward he looked relieved. Almost a year later he contacted me to say that he'd had no more attacks on his health or his family since our prayer time. That was really good to hear. The results had also confirmed to him that the spirit behind the word was not from God. I do not think that all words about God calling people to be faithful in trials are bad or demonic in origin. It was just that this particular word was. That is why we need to pray and ask God for discernment when testing the spirit behind a prophetic word.

Soulish Words

We have talked about words that have the Holy Spirit as their source. We have also talked about words that have demonic spirits as their source. There is also one more kind of word in this category—words that come from our own spirits. "And Peter took him aside and began to rebuke him, saying, 'Far be it from you, Lord! This shall never happen to you.' But he turned and said to Peter, 'Get behind me, Satan! You are a hindrance to me. For you are not setting your mind on the things of God, but on the things of man'" (Matt. 16:22–23). These are words that come from seeing things from a human point of view and not from God's point of view.

Years ago I was praying over people in a prayer line. A young lady came and stood in front of me. When I asked her what she wanted me to pray for she said, "I'd like you to pray and ask God to bless my relationship with my boyfriend." I closed my eyes and waited on the Lord before starting to pray. All of a sudden I heard Him say, "No! I do not want you to bless this relationship. What you bless is blessed and I do not want you to bless this!" I was surprised because I know that God loves to bless people. I opened my eyes, looked at the young lady and asked her to tell me more about her boyfriend and about this relationship. It turned out that her boyfriend was not a believer. While this went directly against the Word of God, she had convinced herself that God would bring him to Christ through their relationship. Sometimes this does happen, but in this case God was not in it. I told her that while God loved her intensely and that He saw her in her loneliness, He would not allow me to bless this relationship. He wanted to be her Lover. When I offered to pray for her for courage to do what she already knew that God was asking her to do she said, "No!" and walked away.

While we can always hear God if we listen, we cannot force Him to say what we, or others, want to hear. As prophetic people we need to be aware of this. It would have been easy for me to assume that because God loves people and wants them to be happy that of course I could bless this relationship. But that assumption would have come from my soul instead of the Holy Spirit.

As I write these words, I realize that some of you reading this book may be married to non-believers. If you are, it is not my intention to condemn you or to make you feel guilty. Marriage is sacred in God's eyes and He can do miracles when you pray.

Other Criteria

There are more questions you can ask yourself to assess a prophetic word. Is the word manipulative or controlling? True prophetic ministry and revelation sets people free to make their own choices. Does the word agree with the principles of Scripture? A lot of prophetic people are telling me these days that God told them that they don't have to go to church anymore. Whatever the reason, this is absolutely not scriptural since it violates Hebrews 10:25: "not neglecting to meet together, as is the habit of some, but encouraging one another, and all the more as you see the Day drawing near." The fact that so many people are getting hurt in churches these days shows us that there is a war around the Church and that the enemy is doing all he can to isolate different members of the body of Christ. It's the same with predators. They isolate an individual animal from the group before they attack it. Everyone who knows Christ is a living stone, but it is only together that we form "the Church."

Finally, does the revelation glorify Jesus (Rev. 19:10b) and does it bring forth the life of God? Even though some things may need to be rooted up and torn down, the end result of prophetic revelation will always be to plant and to build (Jer. 1:9–10).

One of the things we do in our Schools of the Prophets is that we give the students prophetic words that we, or others, have received in the past and we ask them to test them in groups. Here's one of these words.

Case Study
A prophetic word for a local church:

> Get ready church. Get ready! It is now time to act. You need to stop saying that you want to do things for God when you do not act (Ecclesiastes 5:2). Start to move. Do what you've been called to do and stop trying to convince yourself that thinking about acting is the same thing as actually doing it (James 2:14–16). I see a wave and it is getting bigger. It is increasing in height and in power but it's not reaching the shore. It is not because the land is not ready to receive the wave. It is because the wave is not ready to move in such power. The time is coming, however, when that will be the case. Wake up people. Wake up! This wave is meant to reach the shore. "I am ready," says God. "I do not need to increase in power or faithfulness. What happens now depends on you. Your words, deeds and decisions will determine what you see Me do in the future. Be careful what you choose. It does not only depend on Me. It is not, "Our God will do it no matter what we choose." I need you! Without you I cannot move, as you can read in Daniel 7:27, Luke 17:21, 1 Corinthians 4:20 and Revelations 5:10. You rule and reign together with Me. We work together. Position yourselves.

It's really interesting to see the groups in action with the word and there are often heated discussions. Usually half of the class comes to the conclusion that this is from God and the other half that this cannot possibly be from God. The first group does this primarily on the basis of the Bible verses that are included in the prophetic word. The second group does this on the basis of the fact that they are convinced that God is love and that He couldn't possibly say to people "stop trying to convince yourself that thinking about acting is the same as actually doing it." "He would never say that to children who He loves!" they say.

The one thing that everyone does say, however, is that they'd like to know what the pastor of the church for whom this word is meant thought of the word. What was their reaction? This is a criterion that almost no one talks about when it comes to testing prophetic words. It's at this point that I let them know that this word was sent to me in December 2010 by a very prophetic lady who I used to mentor. Our church had been founded only five years before and we were in a very different stage than we are now. Back then I was praying hard. It seemed like no matter what Dick and I did, there was an inertia in the church that made it feel like we were trying to walk forward through molasses. I praise God, however, that this is not the case now.

This word came at just the right time for us and it explained a lot. It explained the feeling of inertia (stop thinking that talking about acting is the same as doing it). The word also encouraged us. We took comfort in the fact that God did indeed want to move in our midst. As we prayed the Lord showed us that we were the wave that He wanted to have reach the land. We saw a movement of people, filled with the Holy Spirit, bringing revival and reformation to our nation and to the nations of the world.

This word was a tipping point for us. We decided that we were not going to bemoan what wasn't happening, but that we were going to act and move forward with those who wanted to go with us. This decision played a key role in us becoming the dynamic church that we are now, with people in different nations of the world all advancing the Kingdom of God in the different spheres of influence of society.

The Role of Spiritual Advisors

I said earlier in this chapter that prophetic revelation needs to be tested for both content and timing. This is where spiritual advisors come in. Even though having spiritual advisors is extremely important, it is also one of the most difficult areas for people to accept emotionally. Time and time again we see this in our Schools of the Prophets. Even after we teach on this subject, as believers, we are so afraid of rejection or of receiving feedback that we do not accept spiritual advisors. We don't like it when people tell us that we may be off in what we're hearing from God. If we're going to learn to work with revelation so that we can see the things that God wants to establish here on the earth come to fruition, we will have to be willing to let God deal with our fears and pride and learn to accept wise counsel.

A young married couple who I knew years ago were really on fire for God and they wanted to serve Him. They'd been praying for God to reveal His will for their lives for a while. One morning the young man woke up and he clearly heard God say that He was calling him and his wife to Africa. Naturally, he was overjoyed. He had finally heard God speak and gotten an answer to his question.

He and his wife came and told me about the experience a few weeks later, and I was happy for them. That is, until I heard what they had to say next. The young husband told me that the same morning God had spoken, he went and sold his shares in the business that he had helped to start to his co-founder and business partner. The next day he and his wife put their home up for sale. It sold two weeks later. This was really quick, and they took it as a sign that God was indeed confirming His will for them to go to Africa.

I said to them, "Africa is a big place. Which country in Africa are you going to go to?"

They said, "We don't know."

I said, "Do you have a mission organization that you'll be working with as you try to find this out?"

They said, "No."

I then said, "What were you thinking? And how in the world are you going to live and provide for yourselves?"

They had been taught that if God speaks you have to obey "immediately" or you're not walking in faith. In the end they did wind up going to Africa—to Kenya, to be specific—where they set up a ministry to help prostitutes become business-women so that they didn't have to prostitute themselves to live. That was two years later. However, in the two years before they left, they were often homeless. This caused a lot of stress for the wife with their young baby. We and many others regularly had to pitch in or they would literally have had nothing to eat. While I respected their desire to live for God, a spiritual advisor could have helped them to process the word from God and make wise decisions about which country they were to be in, what they were supposed to do when they got there, which mission organization (if any), etc.

It's really important that we learn to recognize the people that God has placed in our lives as spiritual advisors and to seek their counsel when processing prophetic revelation, especially the kind that requires us to take action that will have major consequences for our lives. The Bible says that "in an abundance of counselors there is safety" (Prov. 11:14) and that each of us should try to have at least two or three of them.

What constitutes a good spiritual advisor? It is someone you respect, who walks closely with God and who, in addition to knowing the Bible, is able to hear God's voice. This is important because when you go to them for counsel you're not asking them for their opinion. I know from experience that God regularly disagrees with my opinions. It's only as I pray that I get to know His heart on a matter. You're therefore asking your spiritual advisors to pray about what you've shared and to hear what God says to them about it.

A spiritual advisor should be someone who knows you and is willing to make time for you. They should also be someone who has spiritual advisors themselves and is relating to them regularly. If you're married, then your husband or wife is automatically one of your key spiritual advisors if they know the Lord.

An important role of spiritual advisors is to provide confirmation and encouragement about what we think we're hearing from God. We are ultimately the ones that carry the responsibility for the decisions that we make, but spiritual advisors can help us to make wiser decisions based on the revelation that we receive.

One of the questions that I get asked regularly is, "What do I do when I don't agree with my spiritual advisors?" The easy thing to do would be to say, "Who are they to tell me that I'm not hearing from God? Who do they think they are?" I'll give you an example from my own life. As I write these words, Dick and I have been married for twenty-three years. Our marriage partner is the second most important decision that we will ever make in our lives. The most important one is our salvation. Dick and I both know this. This is why when he knew that he had feelings for me he consulted church leaders who he knew were wise and who could hear the voice of God. These leaders also knew him well. I did the same. They were overjoyed for us.

One person whose blessing was crucial to me was my father. My mother had already passed away, but he and my mother had raised me and they knew me better than anyone else. I was in my early thirties at the time. Even though I knew without a doubt that God had spoken to me about Dick, I told him when he proposed that I wanted my father's blessing before we got married. I also said that I was willing to pray and wait as long as it took to get it. I had met and gotten to know Dick in Amsterdam and my father hadn't met him yet.

I'll never forget the moment we exited the airport terminal in Toronto, when my father got his first look at us as a couple. He looked at Dick. He looked at my hand and noticed that I didn't have a diamond ring. He then looked back at Dick. I saw the look on his face and immediately knew what he was thinking, "Hmm! This foreigner wants to marry my daughter and he doesn't even have the decency to get her a diamond engagement ring. We'll see about this!" One of the first things he asked me after greeting us was, "Where is your ring?" It didn't matter how much I explained that the Dutch don't give engagement rings and that I didn't want a ring with a raised diamond, he wasn't having any of it. It was then that I started to pray, because I knew that if God didn't act to change his heart, Dick and I could be waiting a very long time before we got married. Dick also started to pray.

Not everyone would have made the choice that I did. But I figured that if our relationship was from God, then He could and would confirm it to my dad too. We didn't have to wait as long as I expected because God intervened. After going to Canada, we went to Jamaica with my father and my sister to introduce Dick to the rest of the family. Dick shared a hotel room with my dad and I shared one with my sister. A few days after we landed, we went sightseeing. We had lunch at a roadside restaurant that had no walls and that was very popular with the local people. After lunch we got back into the car and drove away.

Forty-five minutes later my sister shouted, "Stop the car! I've left my purse containing all our passports and wallets in the restaurant!" My heart sank because I knew that by now everything would be long gone.

What came out of my mouth at that moment was not "Hallelujah!" I shouted at her and said, "How could you have done that!"

That was when Dick spoke up. He looked at me, my dad and my sister and he said, "Calm down! We are going to pray and then we'll turn back. We will get that purse back. We'll pray that God makes it invisible so that people can't see it."

I had serious doubts, but we prayed and turned around. When we drove up to the restaurant we could see that it was packed full of people. We also saw something else. There, in plain view, was the purse! It was on the ground and we could see it from our car. No one in the restaurant was paying any attention to it. It was like it was invisible to them! Dick got out and picked up the purse. He opened it and found that all our passports and money were there. Nothing had been taken!

From that moment on, my father looked at Dick differently. He saw him for the man of faith that he is. That day he gave us his blessing and Dick became the son my father had never had. Years later, when he called us he'd say, "Hi Arleen. How are you?" And before long he'd ask, "Is Dick home?" I loved it!

These stories show the power of having a spiritual advisor. We choose them because we respect them and the wisdom that God has given them. It is not wise to ignore their advice when they do not agree with us. Prayer works, and through it God can change their hearts, but it also gives Him the chance to change our hearts if He needs to.

CHARACTER

Today's prophets are no longer just mouthpieces who deliver the message. Our lives need to back up the prophetic words that we give to others. This is especially true if God is going to use us in areas outside of the church. We are truly living in times like Joseph and Daniel did. Therefore each of us who desire to be used by God in the prophetic will have to make sure that we allow Him to remove any hindrances (anger, bitterness, rejection, or generational sins) that could distort the revelation that we receive and how we communicate it to others.

CHAPTER 7

Deliverance from Generational Sins

> "And proclaim as you go, saying, 'The kingdom of heaven is at hand.' Heal the sick, raise the dead, cleanse lepers, cast out demons. You received without paying; give without pay."
> – MATTHEW 10:7–8

Several years before Dick and I started Embassy we were part of a team that had planted another church in Amsterdam. This church was open to the move of the Holy Spirit that had started in 1994 in Toronto. It didn't take long before people who had very troubled backgrounds, including Satanic Ritual Abuse (SRA), started coming to us. These people were sincere believers in Jesus Christ, but they had been on a rollercoaster ride for most of their lives. Many of them had gone from one psychologist to another trying to find help, but without success. Every time they took a step forward they would have a setback and wind up being worse off than before.

It was then that we started to cry out to God for help. We knew that if He didn't give us insight into what to do, we would wind up needing as many counselors as the number of church members that we had! God answered our prayers quickly by bringing us into contact with a Christian psychologist who had a lot of experience ministering to people who had been ritually abused. He told us that they had been "healed" by prayer for deliverance from the effects of generational sins.

Several months later he was invited to come to the Netherlands to train us on how to pray for deliverance for these people. Since we'd had no previous experience with praying for deliverance, we knew that we were probably going to make some mistakes as we learned how to do it. It was then that we made the decision, together with the other members of our church's leadership team, to practice by first praying for ourselves before praying for the SRA victims. They had already been so traumatized that we didn't want to make their situations worse. If any beginner's mistakes were to be made, we would rather make them on ourselves.

On the evening that it was my turn to be prayed for, I really expected nothing to happen. I had committed my life to Jesus Christ when I was eight years old. I'd also grown up in a Christian home, and because of this I felt very confident that there were no demons troubling me. The team started to pray and I was peaceful. At one point the Holy Spirit revealed something to them about a specific sin committed by my own family members four generations earlier. All of a sudden things went black as they spoke out in prayer what they saw. That was the moment that I realized that there was something present that I hadn't counted on.

I had been raised in a church where we emphasized that everyone is responsible for their own sins: "all souls are mine; the soul of the father as well as the soul of the son is mine: the soul who sins shall die" (Ezek. 18:4). I knew that each one of us is responsible for our own sins. However, I had never been taught however about the effects of generational curses due to the sins of our forefathers. I had been raised believing one thing, and now here I was being confronted with the effects of something that I knew nothing about.

A particularly powerful verse about the effects of generational sins is: "You shall not bow down to them or serve them, for I the LORD your God am a jealous God, visiting the iniquity of the fathers on the children to the third and the fourth generation of those who hate me" (Ex. 20:5). If we consider that we've all got two biological parents, four grandparents, eight great-grandparents and sixteen great-great-grandparents, there are thirty people whose choices can affect our lives. If even one of them did not know Christ or chose to sin and not own up to it, then the demons will have a "legal right" to come in and oppose us in trying to walk in the fullness of our callings in Christ. That's why we say that every believer needs deliverance from the effects of generational curses on their lives. Another powerful verse about generational sin is, "Our fathers sinned, and are no more; and we bear their iniquities" (Lam. 5:7).

The reality is that both of these truths are true. We are all responsible for our own actions, but the sins of our forefathers, especially if they have not been confessed and repented of, can also hinder us as we try to live for the Lord.

There was no visible demonic manifestation as the team prayed for me that night and I didn't experience any physical discomfort. At the end of the prayer session they commanded the demons to leave me. As they did, I felt a light tingling feeling in my fingers and in my toes. They also did something which we had done from the very beginning of our deliverance ministry. They waited on God for revelation about my gifts and calling.

Each of them got word after word of the prophetic gifting that God had placed on my life. They kept talking about how He was going to use me in this area. Up to that point I had not functioned in the prophetic at all and it is fair to say that no one was more surprised about these words than I was! I did not know where to start, so I eventually wound up praying and saying to the Lord, "God, this is so far from what I expected that I don't know what to do. I'm therefore going to give these words back to You and trust You to fulfill them at the right time." I didn't have to wait long for the answer. This is the testimony that I describe in Chapter 1 of this book with the spirits of "coma" and "deep sleep."

Prophecy, Deliverance Prayer and Inner Healing

I share this testimony because the devil's primary way of working against us is to prevent us from walking in the fullness of our callings in Christ. One of the most effective ways in which he does this is by hindering us in our ability to hear the voice of God, or by causing us not to be able to hear the voice of God at all. Over the past twenty years we and our teams have prayed for more than a thousand people for deliverance from generational spirits, and without exception this is the comment that we hear the most from almost everyone when we're done. They tell us that it's like God turned up the volume and that they can hear His voice more clearly than ever before!

Why does the devil work against us in this way? It's because he knows that when we accurately discern the voice of God, we become truly dangerous to his plans on the earth. Jesus is our example as we have been called to do what He did: "The reason the Son of God appeared was to destroy the works of the devil" (1 John 3:8b).

These days we regard deliverance as a normal and necessary part of the Christian discipleship process. This approach has also played an important role in helping us to create a healthy prophetic culture in our apostolic center. Deliverance from generational spirits is for everyone and our deliverance teams are willing to pray for every believer who wants it. You don't have to foam at the mouth or have a traumatic background.

Since we've started doing this, we've also seen faster inner healing from the emotional pain people had been carrying around, sometimes for decades. The devil is the father of lies (John 8:44) and often emotional pain is held in place by these (unconscious) lies long after the hurtful events have occurred. Wherever there are lies you will also find demons. What we've seen is that when the demons are gone people can be set free from the influence of the power of these lies in their lives. This often goes hand in hand with emotional healing.

Lies in Our Thinking

Often emotional pain is held in place by (sub) conscious lies long after the hurtful events have occurred. For example, many who were bullied as children in elementary school still suffer from the emotional wounds caused by this. "People would reject and hurt me if they knew what I was really like," or "I can't trust people" are just two of those lies. If we don't identify these lies and break their power over our lives, we will reap their consequences.

Lies affect our lives in a number of ways. First, they influence the way that we interpret life. They do this by creating a filter that limits the kinds of information that gets through to us. For example, someone who has an unhealed root of rejection will often think that people are rejecting them even when they're not. The filter of rejection distorts reality and hinders them from forming healthy relationships with others. Someone else who believes a deep-seated lie that they don't deserve to succeed may develop a pattern of quitting their job or of self-sabotaging every time they're about to get promoted.

Second, lies influence how we choose our relationships. The fact of the matter is that often we don't choose our relationships based on what's good for us, but based on our degree of mental, emotional and spiritual maturity. We tend to avoid forming deep relationships with people who are at a different level of maturity than we are. As the saying goes, "Birds of a feather flock together."

Third, lies in our thinking create recurring themes in our lives. For example, a very talented woman I knew got nervous and left every time she had to follow through on something or people started expecting things from her. She believed in the lie that she would be controlled and manipulated if she committed herself to something completely. This fear was based on her past experiences. This was recurring pattern in her life and it was becoming destructive. It prevented her from forming close and lasting relationships and from holding a job or ministry position for longer than a year or two. Every time she left a relationship or a position, she had to start over again. Lies in our thinking create themes that influence the direction that our lives take. What we believe deep inside influences how we think. Our thoughts then influence our actions, and actions if done often enough become habits.

Finally, lies create an inner emptiness. If we don't deal with these lies, we will try to fill this emptiness with things like others' affirmation, money, sex, food or drugs. It's therefore essential that we learn to deal with the lies that we believe. Thankfully, the Lord shows us how to do that: "Don't copy the behavior and customs of this world, but let God transform you into a new person by changing the way you think. Then you will learn to know God's will for you, which is good and pleasing and perfect" (Rom. 12:2, NLT). "Throw off your old sinful nature and your former way of life, which is corrupted by lust and deception. Instead, let the Spirit renew your thoughts and attitudes" (Eph. 4:22–23, NLT).

Demons and Deliverance

Since some of you reading this book may not be very familiar with deliverance and with the whole idea that Christians can have demons, I will spend time expanding on it and showing how we can be free.

Often deliverance evokes images of screaming people and violent demonic manifestations. It is something that most people want to stay as far away from as possible, and it is a ministry that the devil opposes with all his might. He does this in one of two ways. The first is that he promotes ignorance about his existence and about the necessity of deliverance. Many Christians still believe that if we leave demons alone, they will leave us alone. The second is that he causes us to be afraid. Many believers have an almost superstitious fear of demons. Corrie ten Boom, a Dutch woman who hid Jews from the Germans during the Second World War and who went on to become a well-known speaker, once said that "the fear of demons comes from the demons themselves."

Demons are evil spirits that rebelled against God together with the devil. This can be inferred from Isaiah 14:12–15 and Revelation 12:4, where we read a graphic description of a dragon whose tail swept one-third of the stars from the sky. Many Bible commentators agree that the dragon symbolizes the devil, who in his rebellion also turned one-third of the angels against God. These are the stars that were swept out of the sky by the dragon's tail. The Greek New Testament uses the words *daimonion* and *daimon* for "demon." Many times these words are translated as "evil spirit" or "unclean spirit" in English.

As spiritual beings, demons have their own will: "When the unclean spirit has gone out of a person, it passes through waterless places seeking rest, but finds none. Then it says, 'I will return to my house from which I came.' And when it comes, it finds the house empty, swept, and put in order. Then it goes and brings with it seven other spirits more evil than itself, and they enter and dwell there, and the last state of that person is worse than the first" (Matt. 12:43–45). They have emotions: "You believe that God is one; you do well. Even the demons believe—and shudder!" (James 2:19). They are intelligent. In Mark 1:24 we see that the demons understood who Jesus was even before His own disciples did: "What have you to do with us, Jesus of Nazareth? Have you come to destroy us? I know who you are—the Holy One of God!" They also have self-awareness and are able to speak. "And Jesus asked him, 'What is your name?' He replied, 'My name is Legion, for we are many'" (Mark 5:9).

Demon Possession and Demonization

When we talk about demon possession, we mean a situation in which the vast majority of someone's thoughts and actions are controlled by demons. Since Christ lives in each one who has received Him, as Christians we cannot be demon possessed. We can, however, be "demonized." That's a situation in which demons can work against us in a certain area of our lives. Sin is always the key that opens the door to allow demons to do this. Sin gives the demons the "legal right" to bother and harass us. The devil's name means "accuser" and his demons often work by accusing us in our thoughts, attacking our emotions and our bodies with sickness and weakness.

Sin can be divided into three categories:

1. Sin that we have committed.
2. Sin that our ancestors have committed.
3. Sin that has been committed against us causing so much trauma that our spiritual walls of defense are damaged. In this case, lies about our own role in the situation often creep in.

The amazing news is that there is a way out. It says in 1 John 1:9: "If we confess our sins, he is faithful and just to forgive us our sins and to cleanse us from all unrighteousness."

Confession of sin removes any legal rights that demons may have to work against us.

If we ask God to speak to us about sins that we need to confess, He is faithful and He will forgive. In the case of generational sin, however, we may need some help from other believers who are able to hear God's voice. Why? Because we all have blind spots, especially about ourselves.

Deliverance in the Bible

Interestingly enough, there are no examples of demons being cast out of people in the Old Testament. Only when Jesus comes onto the scene in the New Testament does the enmity between the kingdom of light and the power of darkness become evident. We can see the contrast in the following passage: "And immediately there was in their synagogue a man with an unclean spirit. And he cried out, 'What have you to do with us, Jesus of Nazareth? Have you come to destroy us? I know who you are—the Holy One of God.' But Jesus rebuked him, saying, 'Be silent, and come out of him!' And the unclean spirit, convulsing him and crying out with a loud voice, came out of him. And they were all amazed, so that they questioned among themselves, saying, 'What is this? A new teaching with authority! He commands even the unclean spirits, and they obey him'" (Mark 1:23–27). The fact that the demons obey Jesus shows that the kingdom of heaven triumphs over the power of darkness. It did then and still does today.

Our Mandate

Jesus dealt with demons by driving them out of people. The people troubled by demons were mainly God-fearing Jewish people, many of whom He met in the synagogue as He was preaching. Jesus said the following about His own deliverance ministry: "I will keep on casting out demons and healing people today and tomorrow; and the third day I will accomplish my purpose" (Luke 13:32, NLT). The phrase, "today and tomorrow and the third day" is a Hebrew way of saying "from now until the work is done." This means that we are to continue to drive out demons in Jesus' name until there are no more demons left to be driven out. In other words, we are to drive out demons until He returns!

And there are other places where we are called to keep casting out demons, for example: "And proclaim as you go, saying, 'The kingdom of heaven is at hand.' Heal the sick, raise the dead, cleanse lepers, cast out demons" (Matt. 10:7-8). And, "He said to them, 'Go into all the world and proclaim the gospel to the whole creation. Whoever believes and is baptized will be saved, but whoever does not believe will be condemned. And these signs will accompany those who believe: in my name they will cast out demons; they will speak in new tongues'" (Mark 16:15-17).

I mentioned earlier in this chapter that we have prayed deliverance for more than a thousand people in the past twenty years. All of them were Christians who had made a sincere commitment to Christ. One of the most memorable deliverance sessions I ever did, involved a married couple. The wife had been plagued by demons for years, but her husband refused to believe that a Christian could have demons. In order to prove his point, and because she was afraid, he went first. Now in modern-day deliverance, we know we can command demons to show themselves "only as the Lord Jesus Christ allows," as we say in deliverance prayer. That way, you almost always get a quiet session without a lot of the screaming that is usually associated with deliverance prayer. This enabled us to do a lot of deliverance prayer sessions in our home without having to apologize to our neighbors every week. The session with this man was uneventful until he suddenly started screaming. It was loud! Up to that point I didn't know that it was possible for a human being to scream so loudly. Our home has three floors. I was on the ground floor with this man and my team and there was another deliverance session going on in a room on the third floor. The team on the second floor told me later that the screaming sounded like it was in their own room!

At the end of the session I asked the man what happened when he started to scream. He looked at me and said, "All of a sudden I heard myself screaming and I had no control over it. At that moment I knew that I was wrong. I had demons and they needed to leave." His wife then did something that I'll never forget. She started hitting him with her purse. While she was hitting him, she yelled, "Twelve years! Twelve years I've been telling you that I have demons and for twelve years you've told me that I'm wrong because a Christian can't have demons!" He apologized to her and asked her forgiveness for not believing her. Aside from the fact that it was a funny sight, it was also very sad. Fortunately, this story has a happy ending. Shortly after that we prayed for this man's wife and the things that had plagued her for all these years stopped. Her session was one of the few that actually caused me to weep. To this day, seeing Jesus' love and power set her free is one of the most wonderful things I've ever experienced.

If you have never received prayer for deliverance from generational curses (and the associated demons), don't wait any longer. Read, pray and find help![15] It could be one of the best decisions you'll ever make.

CHAPTER 8

Fathers and Mothers, Sons and Daughters

Sometimes we confuse being childlike with being childish. This hinders our ability to grow and to enter fully into God's call for our lives.

One Sunday, Dick was preaching on discipleship. Embassy was new and we were laying the foundations. I was working my socks off, so I was looking forward to getting some help—and soon! Dick and I agreed that during the sermon he would announce that every member was required to have some kind of job in the church. I sat there with a sign-up sheet. When it was time for Dick to make the announcement, I saw him stop. He started to speak, but again he paused. In the end he didn't say anything and my sign-up sheet remained empty.

I was angry because all I could see was more hard work. When I confronted him about it, he told me that God had spoken to him while he was preaching. Just as he was about to say that "every member needs to do a job in the church," he heard the Holy Spirit say, "I don't want you to say that. If every member has to have a job, they are slaves and I don't want slaves. I want sons!"

That experience totally changed our perspective of church life and how we do things. Afterwards we decided we would trust God to speak to people Himself about which job(s) He wanted them to do. We wouldn't ask people, with the exception of certain basic tasks like cleaning up and children's work. It took all the faith we had to trust that God was in this. There was just so much that needed to be done! One couple had a calling on their lives to work with young people and we had to wait for two years before God spoke to them about it. During that time, several families who were considering joining the church decided not to because we had no youth program.

But the effect of this decision was amazing. When people did hear God telling them to do something, they took responsibility and did it much better than we could ever have done. They also didn't get burned out! What we hadn't realized was that by emphasizing every church member's responsibilities, we slowly became performance-oriented. That is what happened in our previous church, where we had been assistant pastors. We had unintentionally created a culture in which people were valued for what they did more than for who they were.

The Father Heart

For an effective prophetic ministry, it's essential to know the Father heart of God. The revelation of God as a Father is at the heart of the New Testament. Jesus Himself was the One who introduced this idea: "When you pray, say: 'Father ...'" (Luke 11:2).

In Luke 15, Jesus tells His disciples several stories illustrating the heart of God the Father toward us. The story of the lost son (Luke 15:11–32) is particularly poignant.

In this parable, the younger of two sons says to his father, "I want my share of your estate now before you die" (Luke 15:12, NLT). In the culture of that day the younger son is actually saying to his father, "Old man, I can't wait any longer for you to die. I want my inheritance now!" This is the ultimate act of disrespect of a son toward his father. The father gives him his portion of the inheritance and the son goes and squanders it. It is only after he winds up starving that he finally comes to his senses.

When he does, he goes home. While he is still a long way off the father sees him, runs to him and embraces him. The younger son has been away for so long that his father didn't know whether he was dead or alive. Before the younger son can finish his pre-rehearsed speech, the father calls for a celebration and the party begins.

Remarkably, when the younger son leaves, the father does not go after him or search for him even though he obviously loves him very much. This is different from what happens in the previous parables, where a shepherd goes after a lost sheep and a woman searches high and low for a lost coin. For a long time I kept asking myself, "Why doesn't the father go after him?" I finally realized that God loves us so much that if we are really determined to, He will let us go our own way. In the parable of the lost sheep, the sheep just wander away. There are so many people who are lost and don't know that there is a God who loves them—and He pursues them! But God, the Father, doesn't force Himself on us. He gives us the freedom to choose what we do. The son in the parable knows the love of the father and deliberately walks away from it. The father continues to love him even after he has gone. But the son does need to make the decision to return. No one else can do it for him. When he does, the father sees him coming and welcomes him back with joy.

The Orphan Spirit

But there is more to this parable. It should really be called the parable of "the lost sons" because there is another son. He hears of his father's party for his brother and is furious. He says to his father, "Look, these many years I have served you, and I never disobeyed your command, yet you never gave me a young goat, that I might celebrate with my friends. But when this son of yours came, who has devoured your property with prostitutes, you killed the fattened calf for him!" (Luke 15:29–30)

It isn't only the younger son who is lost. The older son may still live in his father's house, but he does not experience the father's love. He is suffering from what we call "an orphan spirit." Orphans often feel alone, abandoned and stuck where they are. People with the mindset of an orphan can't experience the joy of being a much-loved son or daughter of their heavenly Father, even though they live in His house. But Jesus tells us that He will not leave us behind as orphans (John 14:18); He wants us to live as beloved heirs.

People with an orphan spirit ...

- are angered when others receive honor. The older brother does not think that his brother is worthy after the mess he's made of things. Orphan spirit traits like jealously, bitterness and envy make it difficult to be happy when others experience breakthrough.
- don't enjoy what they do for God. The older son feels like he has worked like a slave for his father. People with an orphan spirit see serving as an obligation in stead of as something they do out of love (Luke 15:29).
- base their relationship with God on what they do, not on who they are in Christ.
- often distance themselves from those they're angry with. The older brother refuses to go in and celebrate with his father and brother.
- suffer from spiritual blindness. They cannot see the ways God has blessed them and is still blessing them. They do not realize how rich their inheritance is in Christ.[16]

It's obvious that an orphan spirit is not something that we want to carry around with us. And you don't have to. If we ask Him to, God will show us the areas where we are operating out of an orphan spirit.

The Victim Mentality

The victim mentality is closely related to the orphan spirit. It is a pattern people learn in which they see themselves as a victim of other people's actions, and will act accordingly, even if there is no evidence to support their perception. People with a victim mentality tend to believe that others have a negative attitude toward them and they often blame others for the situation they are in. I remember well a lady who attended our church years ago. During a church weekend I saw people trying to talk to her, but she kept excusing herself and walking away. At other times, people started to walk toward her to initiate conversation and she would cast them such an angry look that they stopped and went and talked to somebody else. The interesting thing was that everyone around her was happily talking to each other and making new friends.

At the end of our time together, when I asked her what she thought of the weekend, her reaction surprised me. She said, "It was awful! Nobody talked to me. Everyone rejected me."

When I tried to explain to her what I had noticed, she glared at me and said, "That's a lie. They just don't like me. They all rejected me!" This was one of the first times that I encountered someone with such a strong victim mentality. Shortly after this she told me that she was leaving our church to go somewhere else. What saddened me was that I knew that if she didn't get this issue sorted out, she would encounter precisely the same thing in the next church that she went to.

However, this story has a happy ending. Several years later I met this woman at a conference in another part of the country. She came up to me and let me know that after I had talked to her the Lord Himself started to speak to her about her victim mentality. As a result, she had sought and received emotional healing. What really made me happy was that she had since become a member of a church fellowship and she was enjoying the encouragement and support of close friends there because she no longer believed that people rejected her.

Knowing the Father's Love

There are many ministries devoted to sharing God's father heart, like the Father Heart Schools. For a long time I thought that these were mainly for people who needed pastoral counseling. My reasoning was that we all know that God loves us—that's the first thing you learn when you come to Christ. People with traumatic backgrounds may need extra ministry in this area, but the rest of us are okay. I could not have been more wrong!

During our very first Father Heart School I was translating for the speaker from English into Dutch. The school lasted a week and each day as he spoke, I felt things stirring in my heart. It was as if God was taking the pieces of the puzzle of my heart and rearranging them. By the time the week was done I had received a new heart. God had done a deep work in my heart and healed me—and people noticed it

As I write this chapter, our church has had the privilege of hosting 21 week-long Father Heart Schools. We've seen miracles happen as God heals family relationships, touches His people and sets them free. One lady, attending the school for the seventh time, told me that when she attended her first school she was in a wheelchair. With each school God did a deeper work and now she doesn't need her wheelchair any longer. Her family saw the change in her and, as a result, her husband and all of her children had come to Christ. This time she took her daughter with her to the school.

What we say and prophesy reflects what's in our hearts. If we minister with unhealed emotional pain, our words will reflect that pain. I can often tell what someone's emotional issues are by listening to how they prophesy. Hurting people will hurt other people, whether they mean to or not. It's therefore imperative that we allow the Holy Spirit to minister the love of God the Father to us so that we can be healed. Only then will we be able to speak the words that allow people and nations to be healed.

Childish or Childlike

Jesus spoke a lot about children and the importance of becoming like a child. A key example of this is Jesus' words: "Let the little children come to me and do not hinder them, for to such belongs the kingdom of heaven" (Matt. 19:14). As a result of Jesus' words, I often hear people say that they never want to grow up and that they always want to be children. However, that is not what Jesus meant.

In Genesis 1:28 God commands people to be fruitful and multiply. This is the natural order of things that God has built into creation. Maturity is a prerequisite for pro-creation. In a healthy situation, sons and daughters will eventually become fathers and mothers. However, we don't cease to be sons and daughters when we become physical and spiritual fathers and mothers. Maturity just means that we are willing to carry the responsibility for the people and things that God entrusts to us.

It is crucial that we know the difference between being childlike and being childish. Childishness implies that we are immature. Childlikeness means having the good qualities of a child, such as innocence, honesty and trust. We are called to be childlike but not childish. This is important, because God will not entrust adult-sized responsibilities and riches to those who are immature. It would be like giving your car keys to your four-year-old!

This point was driven home to me a few years ago when a young man approached me after a church service and asked me to pray for his job situation. He had been trying for months to get a better job and had been to interview after interview. Each time he had been turned down even though he had the right qualifications. As I waited on the Lord for insight into what to pray, I heard the Holy Spirit say, "He needs to break the inner vow that he made never to grow up." I opened my eyes and asked him if he had ever made this kind of inner vow. He said that he had. I then asked him to break the vow by saying out loud, "I break the vow that I made never to grow up, in Jesus' name. I choose to grow up and to accept the responsibilities that go with being an adult. Amen." Two weeks later he came and told me that he had gotten a job with a much higher level of responsibility than he had ever had before. There were also a lot of possibilities for advancement. The interviewers told him that "they saw strong management potential in him."

This young man had made the mistake that many who are passionate about the Father heart of God movement unwittingly make. They confuse being childlike with being childish and this hinders their ability to grow and to enter fully into God's call for their lives.

CHAPTER 9

Character before Anointing

Character development is difficult, but it is essential! There are no shortcuts. I'm convinced that God's view about our mountain-top and "valley of the shadow of death" (Ps. 23:4) experiences is radically different from ours. He might well consider our valley experiences to be our mountain-tops.

Throughout the years we have witnessed the fall of some really anointed ministers of God. It hurt their family members, their churches, denominations, and the whole body of Christ. The problem was never with their anointing. It was always with their character. Therefore, when we started God's Embassy, we decided that we were going to prioritize character over anointing. I want to make it clear at the very beginning of this chapter that I am not saying that people have to be perfect in order to prophesy. What I am saying is that for far too long we have put some of God's very anointed sons and daughters on pedestals to the extent that we have been willing to overlook their character flaws. So in our church we try to only give people the size of platform that their characters can handle. We also walk with them to see them healed, restored and set free, so that they can walk in the fullness of what God has for them.

Dick and I have learned valuable lessons by walking with fallen ministers through their processes of restoration with God, their families and the people they lead. First, being in God's presence does not automatically change us. We only change if we choose to embrace God's processes of change in our lives. Second, people can be living in gross sin and still minister under the anointing and power of the Holy Spirit. There was a time when I used to think that this was impossible. Unfortunately, it's not. The Bible says, "For the gifts and the calling of God are irrevocable" (Rom. 11:29). This means that once God gives a gift He doesn't take it back.[17]

Prophetic teacher Lance Wallnau uses a great illustration to explain this process. Our lives are like hot-air balloons. The anointing and the spiritual gifts we receive from God are the hot air that takes us up and increases our influence and our ability to bless others. Our character issues are the sandbags attached to the balloon, weighing us down. They could be things like jealousy, anger and impurity. The list can be long. The more sandbags we have hanging onto the baskets of our balloons, the more we're weighed down and the less we're able to live out the calling God has for our lives. Dealing with our character issues removes the sandbags and allows us to receive what God has in store for us.

Why be so concerned about character? It's because the devil doesn't take us down at the beginning of our ministries. He usually waits until we become better known. That way, a lot more people will be affected. Unfortunately, character doesn't usually get formed when things are going well. Character gets formed in the midst of pain and difficulty, whether it's physical, relational or emotional. The delay between us being hurt or betrayed by someone and the response that comes out of our mouths as a result, is the time in which we can develop our characters.

Character development is difficult, but it is essential! There are no shortcuts. I'm convinced that God has a different view from ours about our mountain-top and "valley of the shadow of death" (Ps. 23:4) experiences. He might well consider our valley experiences to be our mountain-tops.

Let's have a look at two biblical leaders anointed by God to see how God wants to shape character.

Saul

Problems in our lives usually begin long before they become visible to others. King Saul is a good example of this. When Saul first meets the prophet Samuel, he is told that the hope of all of Israel will be placed on him and his family. Saul responds by saying, "Am I not a Benjaminite, from the least of the tribes of Israel? And is not my clan the humblest of all the clans of the tribe of Benjamin? Why then have you spoken to me in this way?" (1 Sam. 9:21). This might look like humility on Saul's part, but it isn't. In 1 Samuel 9:1 we're told that Saul's father was a wealthy and influential man. Saul's words do not line up with the facts. However, Saul is plagued by fear and insecurity and he lets them get the better of him . . . even after God has confirmed by signs that he has chosen him to be the king of Israel. Saul is God's anointed one and yet he is so afraid that he even hides on the day that he is supposed to be crowned as king!

Another problem in his life is his tendency to make foolish and rash decisions. One example is that he ordered his men not to eat while in battle, which made them much weaker than they should have been (1 Sam. 14:24–45). He was impatient and regularly took things into his own hands, and he even consulted a medium (1 Sam. 28).

The sad thing is that Saul does not appear to have someone he allows to mentor him or speak into his life. As a result, these issues are never dealt with.

One day Samuel comes to Saul and says, "The LORD sent me to anoint you king over his people Israel; now therefore listen to the words of the LORD. Thus says the LORD of hosts, 'I have noted what Amalek did to Israel in opposing them on the way when they came up out of Egypt. Now go and strike Amalek and devote to destruction all that they have. Do not spare them, but kill both man and woman, child and infant, ox and sheep, camel and donkey'" (1 Sam. 15:1–3). God gives

Saul and his men victory, but in the end Saul does not obey God. He and his men destroy all that they consider to be worthless, but they keep the best of the cattle. Then God says something shocking to Samuel: "I regret that I have made Saul king, for he has turned back from following me and has not performed my commandments" (1 Sam. 15:11).

So we can actually do things that make God regret His decisions. God loves us so much and regards us so highly that He gives us the freedom to make our own choices, even if they hurt Him. That's mind-blowing and sobering to me. And it just makes me love Him even more. Our choices matter.

About Samuel: the integrity and strength of his character is shown by the fact that after God tells him this about Saul, he cries out to the Lord for him all night.

When Samuel does go to see Saul the next morning, Saul greets Samuel and says, "I have performed the commandment of the LORD" (1 Sam. 15:13). When Samuel confronts him with what he has done, he still does not get it. Unresolved character issues in our lives always lead to spiritual blindness. We call these "blind spots." I was talking to a prophetic minister a while ago about a blind spot in his life. At one point in the conversation he got up, looked at me and said in exasperation, "But how can this be true when I don't see it myself?" Almost as soon as the words were out of his mouth we both started to laugh because at that moment he realized that that's exactly what a blind spot is. It's something that we ourselves don't see. That's why we need others who love us enough to let us know when we have them.

I wrote in the chapter on protocol about the dramatic scene that played itself out between Saul and Samuel at the army camp. In the more than ten years that followed between Samuel's pronouncement that God had rejected him as king and Saul's death, Saul pursues and hunts David, the one on whom God's favor now rests. One of the most tragic things about this story is that Saul's character problems don't just lead to his own demise. Jonathan and his other sons are caught in the fallout and die with him. We never sin in isolation. Sin and our character defects always have an effect on the people we love, and if you're a leader, on those you lead.

David

Before it is David's turn to lead, God tests him for at least thirteen years. From the time he is anointed by Samuel to be king it is obvious to all who were paying attention that he is God's choice. Part of God's preparation process for David is that he allows David to spend years being hunted down by king Saul, who tries to kill him multiple times. Things go from bad to worse. At one point, David even needs to pretend to lose his mind. He lives among Israel's enemies, the Philistines, just to be safe.

Slowly but surely men start to join David. They are thieves and robbers, drunks and dropouts and they live with him in caves, the fields and anywhere they can find. Saul keeps hunting them. The weeks and months pass and the people around see how David endures his trials—not once does David speak negatively about Saul, even though humanly speaking he has every right. They have never encountered anyone like this before and they start to change. Eventually these men grow to love him and they become David's mighty men.

I'm sure there are nights when David, lying alone on his bed thinks back to the moment Samuel anointed him. That seems like a lifetime ago. I'm sure he wonders what happened to his calling and why God is allowing all of this to happen when he is innocent. But he doesn't have too much time to dwell on those things. Just when he begins to get comfortable somewhere, he and his men need to flee again.

David's strength of character is shown by the fact that he spares Saul's life when Saul goes into the cave in the wilderness of Engedi to relieve himself. He could have killed Saul then and there and ended his and his men's exile, but he doesn't. He restrains his men and says, "The LORD forbid that I should do this thing to my lord, the LORD's anointed, to put out my hand against him, seeing he is the LORD's anointed" (1 Sam. 24:6). David could have chosen to become bitter against God, but he doesn't. By the time he leaves the wilderness and becomes king he is a new man. He has become a man after God's own heart (1 Sam. 13:14). I can imagine the angels looking down from heaven as David suffers and runs. They listen as David pours out his heart to God in song and eventually sings his way into all of our hearts. God is faithful, but rarely does He find a man or woman He can really trust. I pray to God that He would make me into someone who He can trust.

The story of these two kings shows that our destinies are not set in stone. We get to choose how we react to circumstances, and our choices have a huge impact on our lives. If David had chosen to become bitter, or even to take Saul's life, his kingship would have been radically different. He would have become a new Saul, not the man after God's heart.

God's Processes

I can't think of a better way to summarize this chapter than by quoting a poem much loved by J. Oswald Sanders, a director of the Overseas Missionary Fellowship in the last century. Its author is unknown.

> When God wants to drill a man,
> And thrill a man,
> And skill a man,
> When God wants to mold a man
> To play the noblest part;

When He yearns with all His heart
To create so great and bold a man
That all the world shall be amazed,
Watch His methods, watch His ways!

How He ruthlessly perfects
Whom He royally elects!
How He hammers him and hurts him,
And with mighty blows converts him

Into trial shapes of clay which
Only God understands;
While his tortured heart is crying
And he lifts beseeching hands!

How He bends but never breaks
When his good He undertakes;
How He uses whom He chooses,
And with every purpose fuses him;
By every act induces him
To try His splendor out—
God knows what He's about! [18]

3

CULTURE

In order for prophecy to flourish in the long-term it has to be an intrinsic part of the culture of our churches and organizations. In this section we'll focus on what that culture is, the role that leaders play in shaping it, and how prophecy in turn influences the cultures in which it is embedded.

CHAPTER 10

The Gospel of the Kingdom

The Gospel of the Kingdom poses challenges to some of our current mindsets; it requires a new way of thinking.

The body of Christ is moving. The Church worldwide is going through major paradigm shifts. One of these is that we are moving from a church-based paradigm to a Kingdom-based paradigm. A church-based paradigm says, among other things, that if we could just plant enough churches and get enough people saved, then society would be changed. That is why it is often referred to as "the gospel of salvation." It also says that if we could just have revival, then everything will change.

Revival, however, was always meant to be for reformation and transformation—it is about more than just salvation. Since what we believe plays such an important role in how we prophesy, I will spend time outlining this Kingdom-based paradigm.

This "Gospel of the Kingdom" is not new. It is an example of "present truth" that God is bringing back to the body of Christ. "For this reason I will not be negligent to remind you always of these things, though you know and are established in the present truth" (2 Pet. 1:12, NKJV). "Present truth" refers to things that have always been in the Scriptures, but that the Holy Spirit illuminates at specific times. This illumination leads to the practical application of these truths by the Church. "The secret things belong to the LORD our God, but those things which are revealed belong to us and to our children

forever, that we may do all the words of this law" (Deut. 29:29, NKJV).
I did not grow up with this mindset. Up until 2004 my view
was that the only two things that are eternal are the Word
of God and the souls of human beings. Everything else was
going to burn up when Jesus returned. Therefore, we needed
to make sure that we got as many people as possible saved
before that. My thinking back then was that "we need to
plunder hell and populate heaven" as fast as possible. While
this is true, it is not the whole story.

My husband and I were deeply impacted at a conference in
The Hague in 2004. There, we heard the American minister
Joseph Mattera talk about the difference between the "gospel
of salvation" and the "Gospel of the Kingdom." As he
spoke, Dick and I turned to each other in utter amazement.
Between us we had been Christians for decades and nobody
had ever explained this to us. That day it was if a light bulb
had been turned on in our minds. Understanding this difference has transformed our lives and our ministry. It has
also had a massive impact on the way I view evangelism, on
how I prophesy and on the way I view the fivefold ministry.

Jesus and the Kingdom

Some of the first words that Jesus said when he began His
ministry were "Repent, for the kingdom of heaven is at hand"
(Matt. 4:17). In *The Passion Translation* it says, "heaven's kingdom realm is now accessible." This means that we don't have
to wait until we get to heaven to see the Kingdom of God in
action here on the earth.

Jesus talked more about the Kingdom than any other
subject. He mentioned it more than one hundred times in
the four Gospels: Matthew, Mark, Luke and John. "And as
you go, preach this message: 'Heaven's kingdom realm is
accessible'" (Matt. 10:7, TPT). Jesus only mentioned the word
"church" three times in these same books. What He was

saying was that He came to make heaven's kingdom realm accessible again to us here on the earth and that we are to demonstrate it now: "You must continually bring healing to lepers and to those who are sick, and make it your habit to break off the demonic presence from people, and raise the dead back to life. Freely you have received the power of the kingdom, so freely release it to others" (Matt. 10:8–10, TPT). We call this message "the Gospel of the Kingdom"—Jesus' power to transform not only individuals, but all of creation, has been delegated to us.

The Gospel of the Kingdom is all-encompassing. The apostle John wrote: "For God so loved the world, that he gave his only Son, that whoever believes in him should not perish but have eternal life" (John 3:16). I had been a Christian for many years before I realized that the Greek word that John used for "world" was actually "cosmos" and not "ethnos." "Cosmos" literally refers to all of creation, while "ethnos" refers to all people groups. Jesus' death and resurrection restored our relationship with God, the Father. But it doesn't stop there!

The Gospel of the Kingdom goes even further. The key to understanding this can be found in the story of creation. "Then God said, 'Let us make man in our image, after our likeness. And let them have dominion over the fish of the sea and over the birds of the heavens and over the livestock and over all the earth and over every creeping thing that creeps on the earth.' So God created man in his own image, in the image of God he created him; male and female he created them. And God blessed them. And God said to them, 'Be fruitful and multiply and fill the earth and subdue it, and have dominion over the fish of the sea and over the birds of the heavens and over every living thing that moves on the earth'" (Gen. 1:26–28). God placed man in the Garden of Eden and gave him the assignment of having dominion over all of creation, with the exception of other people. In other words, Adam was supposed to make the garden look more like heaven. That mandate has never been revoked and it is still our mandate today.

There was, however, a complication. When Adam and Eve disobeyed God (Gen. 3) they gave away their God-given authority and ability to fulfill this mandate. Even though the devil was present in the garden before the fall, he didn't have any authority there. Since he couldn't take Adam and Eve's authority away on his own, he needed them to give it to him. They did this on the day they doubted God's goodness and disobeyed Him. They ate of the fruit of the Tree of the Knowledge of Good and Evil and violated their relationship with God.

Due to the high level of authority that God had given Adam and Eve (they were made in His image), they did not just fall; their act of disobedience subjugated all of creation to the devil's rule. This is why Jesus did not call the devil a liar when he promised Jesus the glory of all of the kingdoms of the world and authority over them if Jesus would just fall down and worship him (Luke 4:6). The devil said, "they are mine to give to anyone I please" (Luke 4:7). Instead, Jesus said, "It is written, 'You shall worship the Lord your God, and him only shall you serve'" (Luke 4:8). The Bible describes the devil as a "roaring lion, seeking someone to devour" (1 Pet. 5:8). He is also called the "god of this world" (2 Cor. 4:4) and "the ruler of this world" (John 14:30). We only have to open our eyes to see the carnage he has caused through things like wars, famine, murder and sickness.

In one sense you could say that Adam and Even suffered from an identity crisis. They were already more like God than anything else in all of creation, since they bore the image of the Creator Himself. The devil was thrown out of heaven for his pride of wanting to be like God: "I will ascend above the heights of the clouds; I will make myself like the Most High" (Isa. 14:14). I can only imagine the horror that he must have felt when he witnessed God creating man and woman. Now the devil was confronted with humankind, which was everything he had ever wanted to be. That's why the devil hates us so much.

The Bible makes it clear why Jesus came. "For in him all the fullness of God was pleased to dwell, and through him to reconcile to himself all things, whether on earth or in heaven, making peace by the blood of his cross" (Col 1:19–20). And, "For the Son of Man came to seek and to save the lost" (Luke 19:10). Jesus came to do more than just save the souls of people. He died to save all of creation from the destruction of sin. This means that Jesus paid the price so that the economies and the governments of our nations could be redeemed. In fact, Jesus paid the price so that every aspect of our world could be redeemed.

Jesus' death and resurrection restored both our relationship with God and our God-given authority to carry out the mandate given to us in Genesis 1:26–28. "And Jesus came and said to them, 'All authority in heaven and on earth has been given to me. Go therefore and make disciples of all nations, baptizing them in the name of the Father and of the Son and of the Holy Spirit, teaching them to observe all that I have commanded you. And behold, I am with you always, to the end of the age'" (Matt. 28:18–20). So we are able to make the earth look more like heaven by demonstrating daily the reality of heaven's realm being accessible now. We are called to cleanse the lepers, feed the poor, heal the sick and raise the dead. And there's more!

The Kingdom of heaven is not just a spiritual kingdom. In Revelation 11:15, the seventh angel blows his trumpet and there are loud voices in heaven shouting, "The kingdom of the world has become the kingdom of our Lord and of his Christ, and he shall reign forever and ever." This idea is backed up elsewhere, "And to him was given dominion and glory and a kingdom, that all peoples, nations, and languages should serve him" (Dan. 7:14). God calls us to reveal the Kingdom of heaven on the earth and He wants to do it now. Therefore, just like we are called to release God's power for healing over sick bodies, we are also called to do the same for sick societies and sick systems in Jesus' name.

A New Way of Thinking

So the Gospel of the Kingdom poses challenges to our current mindsets; it requires a new way of thinking at some points.

First, we saw that the Gospel of the Kingdom is not the same as the gospel of salvation; it goes further. The gospel of salvation is the good news that "if you confess with your mouth that Jesus is Lord and believe in your heart that God raised him from the dead, you will be saved" (Rom. 10:9). Accepting God's offer of salvation restores our relationship with Him. We become part of the Kingdom of God and can start to see the Gospel of the Kingdom in action. God's power starts to flow through our lives to heal us, and through us, to heal our societies.

Second, it's important to exercise our restored dominion over creation. We are to follow in Jesus' footsteps. Throughout His life here on earth He ruled with the heart of a servant and served with the heart of a king. If He did this, then so should we. We are to do so because we love God and we love people.

Third, we were created for earth and not for heaven. The psalmist says, "The heavens are the LORD's heavens, but the earth he has given to the children of man" (Ps. 115:16). Jesus came to earth as a man and showed us what this means. He didn't just preach a "spiritual" message, He also healed the sick, He cleansed the lepers, He raised the dead, He drove out demons and He fed the hungry. By His actions He showed that the gospel is good for body, soul and spirit. In the same way, the Gospel of the Kingdom should impact every area of our lives. It should transform us personally, but it is also meant to transform our families, our work, our educational systems, governments, media and even whole economies. Dr. Abraham Kuyper, the great Dutch Reformer at the beginning of the twentieth century said, "There is not one area of life over which God is not King!"[19] This means that our labor on the earth to transform our societies is not in vain.

Fourth, the Gospel of the Kingdom challenges our eschatology (end time teaching). Within the Church there is a line of thinking that says that the current state of the world is a part of God's plan. As a result, we should wait for the rapture, or for Christ's return, and not try to do anything about the continuing decay of our societies. "To do so would be to work against God's plan," is how this line of thinking goes. But that is not what the Gospel of the Kingdom says. Earth is our home; we are called to transform it. We must let our light shine:

> Arise and shine, for your light has come, and the glory of the LORD has risen upon you. For behold, the darkness shall cover the earth, and thick darkness the peoples; but the LORD will arise upon you, and his glory will be seen upon you. And nations shall come to your light, and kings to the brightness of your rising.
> – ISAIAH 60:1–3

We can't do this if we're just sitting around waiting to be raptured.

Yes, there may be dark times but light always shines the brightest in the midst of deep darkness. Jesus said, "Let me tell you why you are here. You're here to be salt-seasoning that brings out the God-flavors of this earth. If you lose your saltiness, how will people taste godliness? You've lost your usefulness and will end up in the garbage. Here's another way to put it: You're here to be light, bringing out the God-colors in the world. God is not a secret to be kept. We're going public with this, as public as a city on a hill. If I make you light bearers, you don't think I'm going to hide you under a bucket, do you? I'm putting you on a light stand. Now that I've put you there on a hilltop, on a light stand—shine! (Matt. 5:13–15, MSG). We do not have permission to remain passive and hope for the best!

Kingdom Strategy

It is not enough to have a Kingdom theology. We need God's strategy for implementing it if we are to see the complete fulfillment of God's plan. One key contribution to this strategy was given by God to two men. In the 1970s, both Loren Cunningham of Youth With A Mission and Dr. Bill Bright of Campus Crusade for Christ had the same dream. In the dream God showed them the same seven spheres of influence that determine how every society thinks and acts. Loren Cunningham called these areas the "Seven Mind Molders" and Bill Bright the "Seven Spheres." More recently people like Dr. Lance Wallnau and Johnny Enlow have also received the same revelation. They call it the "Seven Mountain Strategy." It outlines seven areas to tackle when initiating nation-changing strategies.

This idea of influencing the Seven Mountains has been shown to be an effective strategy for reforming and trans-forming society—even non-Christians are starting to adopt it. Government leaders, the United Nations and the CEOs of multinational companies are seeing its value. So what does the strategy entail?

Mountains

The "mountains" in the strategy refer to a passage in Revelation. In it, John explains:

> I saw a woman sitting on a scarlet beast that was full of blasph-
> emous names, and it had seven heads and ten horns ... And I
> saw the woman, drunk with the blood of the saints, the blood
> of the martyrs of Jesus. When I saw her, I marveled greatly. But the
> angel said to me, "Why do you marvel? I will tell you the mystery of
> the woman, and of the beast with seven heads and ten horns
> that carries her. The beast that you saw was, and is not, and is
> about to rise from the bottomless pit and go to destruction ...
> This calls for a mind with wisdom: the seven heads are se-
> ven mountains on which the woman is seated.
> – REVELATION 17:3–9

The mountains in this verse are not physical mountains, but spiritual ones. They are the high places, or the systems and institutions that influence mindsets in our societies and they are currently under the control of a world system that is anti-God.

The Bible promises that before Jesus returns, God's mountain will be lifted up above all of the other mountains.

> It shall come to pass in the latter days that the mountain of
> the house of the LORD shall be established as the highest of the
> mountains, and shall be lifted up above the hills; and all the
> nations shall flow to it.
> – ISAIAH 2:2

This is a prophetic promise of a worldwide spiritual awakening that will not only influence the religious sphere, but all areas of society.

The seven mountains are:

1. **RELIGION** – Some call this the church mountain. However, religion includes Christianity, Islam, Buddhism and all other religions. All religions shape people's mindsets and attitudes.
2. **FAMILY** – Parents mostly determine their families' "culture" (atmosphere, norms and values). This has a powerful influence on society.
3. **EDUCATION** – Education shapes how we think.
4. **GOVERNMENT** – Most nations are ruled by government, and this is often the most influential "mountain."
5. **SPORTS AND CULTURE** – This includes art, theater, film and music.
6. **MEDIA** – Media is a key influencer of public opinion. Ideas are promoted by means of social media, newspapers, radio and television
7. **BUSINESS** – Business is possibly one of the most powerful mountains, since this is where finances are generated and the state of world economies is determined.

It is often argued that there are more than seven mountains. Some say that areas such as health care also need to be considered. However, seven is the number of completion. If we use the principles of dream interpretation and God's symbolic language, Bill Bright's and Lauren Cunningham's dream means that all spheres of influence will be impacted.

With the Kingdom theology we have a new missions mandate. We're called to take the gospel to every tribe, tongue, nation *and sphere of influence* on the planet. Winning souls is tremendously important, but it is only the first step in discipling nations. We disciple nations by loving people and by helping them to mature in their relationship with Jesus Christ so that they can walk in God's call for their lives.

Our responsibility comprises three steps. First, we need to get them filled with the Holy Spirit. By prophecy we give them insight into God's call over their lives. And after that we equip them to do what they're called to do, whether that's inside or outside of the walls of the church.

When we do, God's wisdom and power will be released on the government mountain for righteousness and justice. Wisdom, wealth, and generosity will be released through the business mountain, which will fund initiatives, stimulate entrepreneurship and heal nations. Knowledge and competencies will be released through the education mountain for innovation in all areas. Relationships will be restored and parents will receive wisdom to raise up their children to be all that God meant them to be when God's power is released on the family mountain. Art and music will release designs and sounds that up to now have only been seen and heard in heaven. People will have encounters with their Creator and be restored in body, soul and spirit when God's glory is poured out in the mountain of sports and culture. The media will be set free to bring honest and balanced perspectives when God's glory is poured out on the media mountain. All of this will cause the Church to arise and shine and people to come to the light of God's glory.

This is our challenge, this is what it looks like "to disciple the nations." Will we accept the challenge?

CHAPTER 11

Needing New Paradigms

> They will be called oaks of righteousness, a planting of the LORD
> for the display of his splendor. They will rebuild the ancient ruins
> and restore the places long devastated; they will renew the ruined
> cities that have been devastated for generations.
> – ISAIAH 61:3b–4 (NIV)

If we accept that the Holy Spirit gave us the Gospel of the
Kingdom, we must adopt new paradigms and ways of doing
things. God is calling us to shift our thinking because the
ways in which we did things in the past are no longer adequate
to meet the challenges that we personally and in our societies
are now facing.

Breakthrough is Not Victory

A breakthrough (revival) is not the victory. Breakthrough is
a position from which we advance toward the victory (reformation and transformation).

In January 2010, during a period when our church was
fasting and praying for forty days, the Lord gave me a vision,
which illustrates the first change in mindset that we need to
make.[20] In this vision I saw many believers standing on the
border between the wilderness and the Promised Land. They
were celebrating. They had made it through the wilderness
and were ecstatic. They worshiped and they praised God.
Signs and wonders were prevalent. They spent time admiring
the Promised Land from the border and talking about how
wonderful life would be now that they had reached it.

I was surprised, however, when the Lord let me see the border several years later. Memorials had been built there to commemorate the great work of God; as were many churches. Some of these were thriving, but the people were still on the border.

In the end a whole generation lived and died on the border without ever entering the land before them. They had confused breakthrough with victory and had failed to occupy the land. This is a caution to us all. God is saying to the Church it's time to cross over and move forward from breakthrough into victory.

Producing Wealth

Several years ago, Ana Mendez came to Amsterdam to do spiritual warfare against the spirit of prostitution. Within six months the brothels where the prostitutes work started shutting down. A year later, Ana was back. As we walked through the area, I proudly showed her all of the brothels that were now empty. As we talked, she asked me, "Which of these brothels are owned by your church members?"

I was very surprised and said, "Come again? I don't understand what you mean."

She stopped, looked me in the eye and said, "How many of these brothels have been bought by your church members so that they can never be used as brothels again?"

I explained to her that most Christians I knew didn't have the finances to buy something as expensive as a brothel. At that point she poked me in the shoulder, hard, and said, "And why is that? It's because you're not teaching them properly!"

In Chapter 4 I talked about how painful it was for Dick and me when the Senior Pastor of the church we were in before Embassy fell. Money had played a big role in the problems and Dick and I decided we were going to stay as far away from it as possible. There was no way that we were going to mix business and ministry. However, God seemed to have other plans and after my encounter with Ana Mendez, He also sent Dr. Sharon Stone to us to prophesy that God would make our apostolic house a storeroom for financing Kingdom projects worldwide. I had my eyes closed as she was prophesying. Suddenly, I felt her finger poking me in the shoulder—hard. She said, "Arleen, look at me! This means that you and Dick are going to have to learn how to manage money and I mean large amounts of it—tens of millions of euros!" God seems to like to poke me in the shoulder when He's trying to make a point.

These two incidents caused Dick and me to start to study what God really says in His Word about money. If we want to take ground and occupy it, we're going to need a lot of money. While some may continue to receive anonymous envelopes with cash in answer to their prayers, that is not the way that God generally chooses to do things. The Bible says we are given the ability to acquire wealth:

> You shall remember the LORD your God, for it is he who gives you power to get wealth, that he may confirm his covenant that he swore to your fathers, as it is this day.
> – DEUTERONOMY 8:18

Great wealth is being transferred into the hands of the Kingdom-minded believers God has prepared for this task. In the past there were scandals involving high-profile believers who had fallen prey to Mammon. This time things will be different. Only those who have defeated this giant in their own lives will be entrusted with finances at the level to fund the transformation of nations and regions.

Ministry in and to the World

Only 2–3 percent of all believers are called to traditional "full-time ministry" in the church. For centuries, however, our paradigm has been that if you love God and want to serve Him, you have to go to Bible school or seminary and then become a minister or a missionary. Church leaders have taught people that if they are not called to full-time ministry, their primary role is to serve the church as volunteers. Their jobs in the world outside the church are not important; they work to get money to live and to give to the church and various ministries.

The time has now come for us to prepare people for ministry in and to the world. As we do this, some of us may need to go back to school. Do you remember John, the economist mentioned in Chapter 1? He said, "I wanted to go to seminary, but God told me to prepare myself for work in a secular environment." He wanted John to be "like a Daniel in Babylon." God shows us through the prophetic how we can be Daniels. At this tipping-point in world history, government and business leaders find it difficult to know what to do and to set a course. Just like in Daniel's days, God is releasing supernatural levels of wisdom and knowledge to enable us to deal with the challenges of our times. We have been given the mind of Christ (1 Cor. 2:16) and have access to God's wisdom. It's time for us to access it and use it.

Dr. Lance Wallnau was once invited to speak to a group of mega-church pastors in South Korea. Compared to other nations, Korea has a large percentage of mega-churches. During his talk he asked the pastors, "Why is it that I see so many amazing mega-churches in this nation, but this isn't reflected in the same way in business here? There are very few multinationals started and run by Christians compared to the number of mega-churches."

The pastors were silent for a very long time. Lance thought that the pastors had possibly not understood the question, so he repeated it. When the pastors were silent a second time, he asked the translator what was going on. The translator told him that the pastors had understood the question and that they were thinking hard about the answer. Finally, the leader of the group stood up. He was a very highly respected pastor and had the largest church of the group there. He looked at Lance and said, "I would like to answer this question. I have just realized that it's because for years we have pulled the brightest and the best of these people into the church instead of encouraging them to go out into society." He then repented for this before God on behalf of the group.

When he was done, a young man stood up. He was a youth pastor in another church. He said, "I need to repent of something too. Years ago, as a young believer, I went to my pastor and told him that God had called me to be a future president of our nation. When I went to my pastor at the time to tell him this, he told me that I needed to repent of my pride and arrogance and for even thinking that I could do this. He then told me that I should go into the ministry. I want to confess here and now that I have not been true to my calling."

Lance then said that the group of men present gathered around this man and prayed for him. At the end, one of them said, "Young man, you need to go back to school and when you've completed your studies, I'll be happy to finance your campaign when you run for president!"

Shortly after hearing Wallnau tell this story, a lady who was new to our church came to me and said, "I'm so angry! During the past three years I've turned down six promotions at my work. Every time I talked to my pastor about whether or not I should accept the promotion he said,

'A promotion would mean that you would have to spend more time at work and that you wouldn't have time to lead the women's ministry and my Bible study group.' I realize now that I should have said yes to the promotion because God has called me to bring His Kingdom to the business mountain!" These days Dick and I spend a lot of time discouraging people from going to Bible school. It's not because we are against Bible schools. It's because these people are not called to the religion mountain. Instead, we help them to discover which mountain they are called to. We then equip them and set them free to move into it.

Revival is Not Enough

Revival must be combined with reformation if we're going to see long-term transformation of both individuals and the world we live in. We've often thought that everything in the world would be all right if we could just have revival. Then people would get saved and society would change. This assumption is based on the idea that if we could just get enough people saved, society would change on its own. In other words, "Transformed people transform society." But this is not supported by the facts. Transformed people only transform the world around them if they know that they're supposed to and if they're equipped to do it!

This became painfully clear to me last year during our Economic Summit Africa (ES Africa) meeting in Cape Town. The speaker was a godly lady with a strong faith in Christ. Her words, however, shocked everyone in the audience. She said, "All you people from the West, please stop holding your big evangelism campaigns in my country! We are 85 percent Christian in my country and we are a mess. Our crime, murder and corruption rates are sky high. We don't need more Christianity. We need more Christlikeness!" Unfortunately, the same can be said of many nations. Christlikeness is the result of discipling people to display the Kingdom of God through their character and their actions. We are called to live out the love of Christ and to bring God's solutions to every single one of our spheres of influence. When we do, we will see society change.

When revival doesn't lead to reformation, it leaves societies worse off than they were before. Revival cleans up the spiritual atmosphere of our cities and nations. When we subsequently do not occupy the "mountains" or spheres of influence of our societies, the original demons that were there come back and they bring their friends with them. What Jesus taught about this subject is also true of cities and regions: "When the unclean spirit has gone out of a person, it passes through waterless places seeking rest, but finds none. Then it says, 'I will return to my house from which I came.' And when it comes, it finds the house empty, swept, and put in order. Then it goes and brings with it seven other spirits more evil than itself, and they enter and dwell there, and the last state of that person is worse than the first. So it will be with this evil generation" (Matt. 12:43–45).

This is why most revivals are short-lived and the benefits that they bring to society are equally short-lived or completely absent. Revival is necessary and it is meant to revive the Church. When we see the signs, wonders and miracles that accompany revival they awaken a new level of faith in us. But revival is meant to lead to reformation and reformation to transformation. When we do not train people to look beyond revival and bring about transformation, it's like cleaning up the house but not occupying it with something else. That's why often after revival ends a city will not only revert back to its original state, but it will be much harder to win it for Christ and to see revival come again.

Some of us still remember the Transformation video series that George Otis Jr. produced years ago. In the first video he told the story of Almolonga, Guatemala. It was an impoverished town with a lot of crime that experienced a powerful revival. Thousands gave their lives to Jesus and some of the prisons had to be closed because hardly anyone was committing crimes. This revival even affected the land that was used for agriculture. It became fruitful and the fruits and vegetables that it produced were huge in size. The economy of Almolonga experienced a turnaround and the city became prosperous because of this.

However, a few months ago I spoke to someone who told me that he had just been to Almolonga. He went because he wanted to see what the revival there was like now. What he discovered shocked him. All of the prosperity that they had experienced was gone. Poverty was back and the government was having to build new prisons to house all of those who were committing crimes and being convicted! This is what happens when we do not teach people to go from revival to transformation.

Discipling Nations

Evangelism will always be an important part of our mandate as Christians. But there needs to be a change in thinking: evangelism alone isn't enough. We need to disciple nations.

A few years ago, when Reinhard Bonnke held his evangelistic campaigns in Nigeria, millions of people committed their lives to Jesus Christ. I still remember watching video fragments of a meeting and being awestruck as I saw the Holy Spirit fall on tens of thousands of people at the same time. I have friends who know the areas Bonnke went to in Nigeria well. They tell me that almost immediately after the meetings ended, Muslim groups went into the areas where the meetings were held and started businesses that provided work for the local population. After a while, there were so many of these businesses in an area that the business owners could demand schools in which the Koran was taught to their children. In addition to the schools, mosques were also built. Eventually, the businesses, the schools and the mosques began to exert so much influence that many of those who had given their lives to Christ began to feel that while Jesus was able to save their souls, Allah was the one who helped them to put food on the table and provide a future for their children through education.

My husband and I travel regularly to Mozambique. The north is predominantly Muslim, but the south is considered to be Christian. The last time we were in the southern town of Maputo, however, we saw exactly the same thing happening there. A city that was a hotbed of revival not so very long ago was now well on its way to becoming a Muslim city. Muslims are using a kingdom strategy. Shouldn't we Christians do what they do? Shouldn't we follow the command that Christ gave us: win souls and disciple nations in His name?

For many, demonstrating the Kingdom of God on the earth is all about obeying Christ's command in Matthew 10, cleansing the lepers, healing the sick and raising the dead. In other words, we are to demonstrate Christ's power to heal our physical bodies. And we're certainly supposed to do this, but sometimes we become so focused on personal miracles that we miss the bigger picture. When the Bible describes the tree of life, it says that its "leaves . . . were for the healing of the nations" (Rev. 22:2). God wants to heal nations! This means that just like we are called and anointed to heal sick bodies, we are also called and anointed to heal sick economies, political systems, educational systems and nations.

And you know what? You don't need a majority to heal nations and transform culture. That is good news, especially for nations where Christians form only a small minority of the population. A good example of this is the Jewish people. They have never formed more than 3 percent of the population of the nations where they have lived, with the exception of Israel, and yet they have had an influence throughout history that far exceeds their numbers. While Jews only make up 0.2 percent of the total world population, they have won at least 20 percent of all Nobel Prizes since 1901.[21] In the United States 10 percent of all of the university professors and researchers are Jewish, even though they only make up 1.8 percent of the total population[22] and the list goes on.

New Words

When God gave me the idea for the Economic Summit He said very clearly that it was not to be a "Christian business and economic summit" but a "business and economic summit run by believers who were Holy Spirit-filled and who were passionate about Jesus Christ." It still surprises me at times how many of us think that when we're in secular circles that we have to emphasize that "we are Christians!" In no way am I advocating being ashamed of the gospel. However, if you are called to work in the marketplace, God may lead you into an arena where being overtly "Christian" will be an unnecessary hindrance to you accomplishing God's plan. It is a religious idea that as long as we say "I'm a Christian" at the beginning and the end of every conversation, this is going to bring people to Christ.

Again and again I see people coming to Christ because of the testimony of those who know Him in word and in deed. I was recently in Leeds, England to do some prophetic consulting for a business. They had to make some strategic decisions about how they were going to grow and expand in the future. After spending the day with them listening and giving them what I felt was the word of the Lord for their situation, they invited me to speak to and to pray for their employees that evening. I ministered to everyone there and gave them a prophetic word. At the end of the evening they asked one of their administrative assistants to drive me back to my hotel.

As we drove she shared with me about her family and her background. She hadn't had an easy time. "But," she said, "my life changed when I came to work for this company. They do what they do really well and they really care about people. They helped me to find a new place to live when the owner of the house that I was renting decided to sell it suddenly and they gave me time off with pay when my children were going through a bad patch." As I listened, I felt proud of my friends. They didn't just speak about what they believed, they acted on it as business owners. She then went on to say, "I so want to believe what you prophesied over me. I know that I must be here for something, but I don't know how to start!"

I realized that she didn't yet know Jesus Christ and said, "Well, since God created you and gave you this calling, the best place to start would be to get to know Him." I then asked her, "Have you ever given your life to Jesus?"

She said, "No."

So I said, "Well, why don't we do that right now? Would you like to?"

"Oh yes! I really would."

That night when we got to the hotel, I was able to pray with her and lead her to Christ. As she prayed, she sat there and wept tears of joy. My work was easy. My friends had already prepared the way with their work.

Winning people to Christ will always play a central role in what we're called to do. There is no disconnect between evangelizing and leading people to Christ. In the reality of the new global marketplace, however, walking our talk is also crucial.

CHAPTER 12

On the Foundation of Apostles and Prophets

> And he has appointed some with grace to be apostles, and some with grace to be prophets, and some with grace to be evangelists, and some with grace to be pastors, and some with grace to be teachers. And their calling is to nurture and prepare all the holy believers to do their own works of ministry, and as they do this they will enlarge and build up the body of Christ. These grace ministries will function until we all attain oneness in the faith, until we all experience the fullness of what it means to know the Son of God, and finally we become one perfect man with the full dimensions of spiritual maturity and fully developed in the abundance of Christ.
> – EPHESIANS 4:11–13 (TPT)

Since the Reformation, the Church has primarily run on three types of ministries—the pastors (those with shepherding gifts), the teachers and the evangelists. They have worked with dedication and enthusiasm, but something is missing. The Church worldwide is at a crossroads: just doing what we've always done is not going to bring us further. We need to acknowledge that God has also given apostles to the Church today. Without them, we will not be fully equipped and the Church will not mature adequately. Nor will we see the unity for which Christ prayed so fervently before He went to the cross (John 17:20-23). Without apostles we will continue to be anemic and not be able to walk in the fullness of all that Jesus meant us to be. Also, without apostolic leadership, the prophetic will not be able to effectively do what it's supposed to do: to bring breakthrough.

Before I go into why apostles are so important and why prophets need to work together with them, I'll talk about the three ministry gifts that we're most familiar with, namely the pastors, teachers and evangelists.

Pastors

Even though pastors—people with shepherding gifts—have played such a dominant role in the Church since the Reformation, the word "pastor" is only mentioned once in the entire Bible (Eph. 4:11). In stark contrast, the word "apostle" is mentioned eighty-eight times in the New Testament.[23]

The office of the pastor is first and foremost an anointing from God that causes people to want to shepherd God's flock. The pastor's constant focus is the local church, and their entire life is interwoven with their congregation. The pastor has God's heart to shepherd and to care for His people. This anointing breaks the bonds of isolation and independence. A pastor causes people to feel safe and to congregate with each other within the body of Christ.

There can be many people with a shepherding anointing within the church. For example, someone may have a heart for children. The presence of the anointing will cause children to be supernaturally attracted to that person. I'll never forget one of the first times that the man who leads our children's ministry taught Sunday school. In his daily life Gert-Jan is an advisor to the Board of Directors of one of the Netherlands's largest banks. Before that I'd never seen him in anything except a suit and a tie. That morning, he taught about 1 Samuel 20. A quick recap: David is hiding from King Saul and Jonathan has found out that Saul wants to kill David. Jonathan and David have agreed that if Jonathan shoots his arrows past the place where David is hiding, David will know that it isn't safe for him to remain in Israel. Gert-Jan brought in sticks and branches and had the children make their own bows and arrows. After the service I happened to be standing in the foyer when he came downstairs. At that moment he was the Pied Piper to the children that he had taught. Twelve young boys were walking behind him with their self-made bows. They were jumping up and down as they walked and kept asking, "Can you please come and teach us again?" None of the other leaders of the children's work before that had ever gotten that kind of reaction. That was the day that we knew that we had appointed the right person for the job.

Teachers

The office of the teacher is different from the natural talent to teach that many have. It is an anointing from God that imparts a powerful motivation to people to want to help others to understand the principles of God's Word and to avoid error. The teaching anointing doesn't just instruct, it also sets people free from sin, depression and destructive behaviors through the opening up of God's Word: "So Jesus said to the Jews who had believed him, 'If you abide in my word, you are truly my disciples, and you will know the truth, and the truth will set you free'" (John 8:31–32). The Spirit of Truth works through the teacher. We used to have a friend who was an anointed teacher. Every year when he went on vacation he would bring along books on theology and other areas of doctrine. The first thing that he did when he and his wife got to camping grounds was to stake out a picnic table. For large parts of his vacation he could be found there thoroughly enjoying poring over these books and commentaries.

Evangelists

The word "evangelist" (*euangelion* in Greek) means someone who "brings good news." The main aim of the evangelist is to help people come to salvation in Jesus Christ. The cry of the heart of the evangelist is to motivate other believers to go into the whole world and to preach the gospel. I remember my conversation with a dear man of God who has a vision to evangelize Europe. As I was telling him about what we as a church did, he looked at me perplexed and said, "Arleen, it's all about bringing people to Christ. If you are not doing this, you're just wasting your time!"

The anointing of the evangelist supernaturally causes people who don't know the Lord to respond to the preaching of the Gospel of Salvation.

Apostles

One of the great rediscoveries of our age is God's plan with apostles. In a way, it's surprising that the Holy Spirit has had to point it out once again; the Bible has made it clear all along.

Before I start to describe the apostolic anointing, I want to address the fact that many are wary of the high level of spiritual authority that apostleship carries with it. Because of that, they may deny the existence of modern-day apostles in the Church. But apostles can be found in Church history —along with the prophets, they are the ones who have suffered most for the Church. I was reminded of this when Dick and I were at an exhibition of Rembrandt's paintings. Among the paintings there were two of the same man. The title was "Apostle Bartholomew before he was skinned alive." In one of those, Bartholomew holds the knife that is used to do this. I couldn't take my eyes off of the man's face. I felt like I could see the shadow of death in his eyes. It was chilling and remarkably sad at the same time. It was clear that he had resigned himself to death for the Church that he loved and for the mandate that God had given him. That picture haunted me for months afterwards and I don't think that I'll ever forget it. These days when I teach on apostles, one of the first things that I say is that yes, they possess a high level of spiritual authority, but they also carry greater responsibility. Many apostles suffer for the Church; some will even die for it.

One example of a historical apostle is Dutch theologian, pastor, politician and journalist Abraham Kuyper. Many people, especially in the United States, consider him to be the original Seven Mountain man. Throughout his life he worked tirelessly to reform Dutch Protestantism (religion mountain). He founded a national newspaper (media mountain) to influence public opinion. He established a political party based on Protestant Christian beliefs and was Prime Minister of the Netherlands from 1901-1905 (government mountain). He also started the *Vrije Universiteit* (Free University) in the Netherlands (education mountain) and was responsible for getting a law passed which allowed Christian schools to receive government funding. This law is still in effect today. Abraham Kuyper is undoubtedly one of the Netherlands' most famous apostles. Suffering comes in many forms and like all pioneers, Kuyper had to fight many battles in each of the mountains God called him to. It's not without reason that the apostle Paul associates an apostolic calling with perseverance (2 Cor. 12:12).

The Greek word for "apostle" (*apostolos*) means "sent one." An apostle is someone who is sent by God; someone with an assignment. Paul emphasized this in his introduction to the book of Galatians: "This letter is from Paul, an apostle. I was not appointed by any group of people or any human authority, but by Jesus Christ Himself and by God the Father, who raised Jesus from the dead" (Gal. 1:1, NLT). Apostles can be recognized by the high level of spiritual authority that they carry: "The signs of a true apostle were performed among you with utmost patience, with signs and wonders and mighty works" (2 Cor. 12:12). Mature apostles are also men and women of high character: "For we are not, like so many, peddlers of God's word, but as men of sincerity, as commissioned by God, in the sight of God we speak in Christ" (2 Cor 2:17). Their lives exemplify Christlikeness: "We put no obstacle in anyone's way, so that no fault may be found with our ministry, but as servants of God we commend ourselves in every way: by great endurance, in afflictions, hardships, calamities, beatings, imprisonments, riots, labors, sleepless nights, hunger; by purity, knowledge, patience, kindness, the Holy Spirit, genuine love" (2 Cor. 6:3–6). Apostles are also people of great faith: "We are confident of all this because of our great trust in God through Christ" (2 Cor. 3:4, NLT).

The Greek word for "missionary" has the same root as that of "apostle." However, a missionary can only be said to be an apostle if they demonstrate the spiritual authority and the works of an apostle. Apostles are called to plant, to initiate, lead and mentor. One of their main desires is to set people free to walk in God's calling on their lives. Apostles think big. Their vision is bigger than just the institutional Church. Apostles may be called for geographical areas and for the Church, but also for the marketplace and for the different spheres of influence in society.

People with a shepherding anointing have difficulty setting people free and letting them go because of their strong desire to protect them. In the shepherd's mind there is always something else that needs to be healed in the person's life before they're ready to be sent out. Shepherds need apostles to help them to accept the fact that people don't always need to be completely healed before they're let loose on the world. After a certain point, their healing will continue as they move out to do what God has called them to do.

Paul wrote that in God's order it is first apostles, then prophets, then teachers (1 Cor. 12:28). This explains why people with apostolic and prophetic anointing tend to struggle under church leaders who are teachers or shepherds. A friend of ours who pastors a large church in the city once asked, "Dick, what do you do with all of your talented young people? We have a lot of people graduating from Bible school, but I have nowhere to put them. I already have a worship leader and a Sunday school leader." Dick was utterly shocked. This man may have been a gifted shepherd, but his paradigm was limited to what people could do in his church. He never even considered that God might have more use for them outside the church walls! Since most of our churches are led by teachers and shepherds, many with apostolic and prophetic gifting are exiting the church. But if the apostolic functions correctly, apostles can ensure that barriers to people's development disappear.

Apostles and Prophets

This book is called *Impact* because I believe that prophets and prophetic people must learn how to move beyond just speaking out our prophetic words, to learning how to impact society with the revelation that God gives us. It's God's desire that we practice what He reveals to us in our society. He wants to give innovative ideas for fashion and concepts for new television programs that reshape the way people think. He has new ideas for business and education and even for ending poverty.

Apostles and prophets lay foundations and are both able to "build," but they do it in different ways. The prophet does so by speaking out God's purposes for what He wants built and by calling it forth. The apostle roles up his or her sleeves and gets to work building it. The anointing of the apostle is both visionary and practical. Apostles are the ones who build in such a way that things are revealed and become visible on the earth (Rom. 15:20). As prophets it is therefore crucial that we learn to work together with apostles. If we don't, our prophetic words will remain largely that—just words. The Spirit of God is saying that it's time for things to materialize!

In the past, apostles and prophets have tended to clash, mainly because they have different personalities. I am a prophet and I am married to an apostle. My role is usually to say, "We're called to go in this (or that) direction and we're called to do it *now*!" Dick will often say, "I agree with the direction, but first we need to do this, and then that, and then something else." I used to get frustrated with him because I thought that he was dragging his feet. I now realize that there was often wisdom in his approach and that when we do things together, we build things that last. We've learned through experience that when one of us doesn't have peace about something it is folly for the other to ignore it. A lack of peace indicates that either the timing or the direction is off.

In the British city of Bath, there is a group of apostolic leaders I've been privileged to work with. They've been meeting for several years to build relationships with each other. In that time, God has given them a vision for the city that is bigger than themselves. After I spoke at one of their monthly meetings, they asked me to help them form a prophetic and an apostolic council for the city. They did this because Dick and I have experience with city transformation in Amsterdam. Besides that, I have learned as head of the Netherlands Prophetic Council that prophets thrive if there is a team of apostles to share their revelation with.

The apostles are able to come alongside them and make sure that the words materialize, by making them practical.

In Bath, we now meet as an apostolic council during the mornings, and we invite prophets in to join us for the afternoons. This approach works well for at least two reasons. First, the prophets and apostles get to know each other, creating mutual trust. Second, they have a chance to receive revelation from God together. As the prophets speak it out, the apostles can test it immediately, and those things that make it through the testing process can usually be implemented pretty quickly. This has proven to be a model that works well. The prophets are able to see that they are taken seriously and that their words are acted upon, and the apostles get the revelation that they need. In the final chapter of this book I will give a few examples of apostles and prophets working together, through divine revelation, to bring breakthrough and transformation to people's lives, workplaces and cities. This is what it means to have an impact.

CHAPTER 13

Impact

> Revelation is supernatural, but not airy-fairy. It is powerful, and as we work with it where God has placed us, His Kingdom will be demonstrated because His will is being done on earth as it is in heaven.

It's great when God does signs, wonders and miracles through the prophetic. Each story of God's intervention is special; we should celebrate all that He does.

Just today, I saw how God encourages people at just the right moment. I received an email from a business leader in Israel I had prophesied over earlier in the day. He wrote: "Dear Arleen. Thank you so much for being a channel for the Word of the Lord. You have no idea how many deep things in my heart your word touched. Clearly it was the Lord, because through you issues were addressed that I've long dreamed of and discussed with the Father over the last two decades."

In this last chapter I share stories about how God works through revelation to bring breakthrough to people's lives. Each story illustrates something that is relevant to us all.

Revelation is supernatural, but not airy-fairy. It is powerful, and as we work with it where God has placed us, His Kingdom will be demonstrated because His will is being done on earth, as it is in heaven.

Housing the Apostolic Center

Years ago, soon after we started Embassy, we were looking for a building to rent that could serve as a base for our apostolic center. At that time we were meeting in a YWAM building called De Poort. While we appreciated YWAM's hospitality, we really wanted a place of our own. As I was praying about this one day the Lord spoke to me and said, "What are you doing?"

"What do you mean, Lord?" I asked.

"Did I tell you to go and look for a building to rent?" the Lord asked.

"No, You didn't," I said.

"Then just start reaching out to the neighborhood and don't worry about the building," He said, "I'll let you know when it's time."

As a result of this encounter we gave up looking for a building and just got on with things. We wound up doing a lot of evangelism in the Red Light District and saw many people come to Christ.

Five years later, Dick was praying in YWAM's House of Prayer in the Red Light District. Every week, a group of pastors from the city gathered there to pray, but on this particular day Dick was on his own. While praying, all of a sudden he heard God's voice say, "Tell Me where you want the building."

"What, Lord!?" said Dick.

The Lord repeated Himself, "Tell me where you want the building."

Dick took a map of Amsterdam, laid it on the ground and said, "I want it here." We didn't want a traditional church building, but a multifunctional facility that was close to metro and train stations. It also had to have easy access to the city center and the airport. That was quite a list of requirements! When Dick shared that with me, God confirmed to me that it was indeed Him who had spoken.

Once more, we started to look for a building to rent in the general area that Dick had asked for. I thought that since

God had spoken, things would be easy . . . but that was far from how things turned out. After two years of searching and six rejections to our offers to rent properties we didn't know what to do anymore. Sometimes we were told flat out: "You're Christians and we don't want you in our building!"

Around that time we had a Canadian prophet speak at our Sunday service. During her sermon she said, "Dick, God says you and Arleen should be looking in a different part of the city. Expand your search area and look for the building in a different part of town."

Two weeks later, one of our church members asked, "So, are we going to start to look in different parts of the city for the building?" Dick and I answered by saying that so far, there had only been one word saying that we were looking in the wrong place. All of the other words from prophets who we knew had confirmed that we were looking in exactly the right place. We assured the church that we would take the word seriously. We would, however, ask God to confirm it before we changed our search criteria.

This is an important principle in building with the prophetic. If you know that God has spoken to you, do not change your direction on the basis of a single prophetic word from someone else. Always ask God to confirm the new word again before you start off on what could be a long rabbit trail. People have suffered serious consequences in the past by not doing this:

> Then he said to the man of God, "Come home with me and eat some food."
>
> "No, I cannot," he replied. "I am not allowed to eat or drink anything here in this place. For the LORD gave me this command: 'You must not eat or drink anything while you are there, and do not return to Judah by the same way you came.'"
>
> But the old prophet answered, "I am a prophet, too, just as you are. And an angel gave me this command from the LORD:

> 'Bring him home with you so he can have something to eat and drink.'" But the old man was lying to him. So they went back together, and the man of God ate and drank at the prophet's home.
>
> Then while they were sitting at the table, a command from the LORD came to the old prophet. He cried out to the man of God from Judah, "This is what the LORD says: You have defied the word of the LORD and have disobeyed the command the LORD your God gave you. You came back to this place and ate and drank where he told you not to eat or drink."
> – 1 KINGS 13:15–22 (NLT)

So if you're in doubt about whether or not God is telling you to do something different than what He originally told you, you should always go back and ask Him to confirm it.

A month later, Bishop Bill Hamon and Sharon Stone were with us to speak at a conference that we had organized. Bishop Hamon prophesied, "Dick and Arleen, Christmas is going to come early this year with regard to contacts that will lead to the new building that you have been looking for."

Sharon nudged me and said, "You need to pay attention to this! That's the first time I've heard him mention a date in prophecy in the past ten years!"

I'll never forget that word. On December 21st I was having my time with the Lord. I remember clearly saying to Him, "Lord, remember the word that Bishop Hamon spoke out? Well, Christmas is December 25th and we're still waiting for that contact." On December 22nd we got the phone call. It was from the two men who had been helping us search for a new building. They said, "Dick and Arleen, we've found a building! It's really close to where you live and it's not only for rent, but also for sale. We think that you have enough money to buy it."

We called the realtor and set up an appointment to see the building on January 3rd. Immediately we saw the potential and we put in an offer on the building. It was in exactly the area that Dick had been praying for! It was also at least twice as big as anything we'd seen up to that point. We bought it, and these days we've got a building that can hold more than 1,000 people, that is fifteen minutes by train from the airport and just ten minutes away from the city center by metro. That was the first time in many years that a church, any church, had been able to buy a building. These days it's not unusual for us to get visits from pastors and the leadership teams of other churches asking us: "How did you do it?" and our story has helped several of them to get their own multi-functional buildings. But boy, were we glad we didn't change our search criteria!

The Role of the Apostolic

You could read this story and think, "Praise the Lord! Isn't it wonderful how God works? He gave a prophetic word and it was fulfilled." While this is true, there were practical steps that needed to be taken before we were able to buy the building. First, as a church we needed to save half a million euros (about 500,000 USD) in the first five years of our existence. This was only possible because when the church offered to pay Dick a salary he said, "No! I've got my own company. I like what I'm doing. Instead, put the money in a savings account in a bank. Who knows? Maybe God will allow us to buy a building one day." Even now, Dick is still bi-vocational, although our church has grown considerably since then. We have an amazing leadership team, and due to our empowering culture, neither he nor I have to spend the majority of our time on the church.

While the Bible definitely says that "those who work deserve their pay" (Luke 10:7; 1 Tim. 5:18), but church leaders and missionaries worldwide are having to re-evaluate how they get their wages. I'm not exaggerating when I say that we've known missionaries who have had to live on peanut butter and jelly sandwiches for the last week of each month because they haven't been able to raise enough support to be on the mission field ... and all of this happens while they have college and university degrees that would allow them to work part-time.

The world is changing and we're going to have to look again at how we finance ministry. If God is emphasizing anything right now, it is the role of marketplace ministers in bringing the Kingdom of God into every sphere where He places them. Both Dick and I see bi-vocational ministers as the future for many churches. Often, pastors want to go on salary as soon as the church is able to pay them. The result of doing this too soon is often that churches remain small, simply because they don't have enough money to initiate projects and programs. It also causes them to become isolated from the world around them that doesn't know Christ, since much of the time they're busy with "the church." Bi-vocational ministry solves these problems and is also biblical (2 Cor. 12:13–14, TPT).

While the prophetic helped us to identify the building, the practical approach of the apostolic actually allowed us to buy it. Both were needed.

Our Choices Matter

We used to think that if a word was from God then He would fulfill it on His own. We didn't need to do anything. Now we know better.

Years ago when we started the church, one of our members was a very gifted musician. He played the violin, and he did so beautifully. This man had received many prophetic words that he would record an album. One day this man was diagnosed with cancer. He had chemotherapy, and on a short remission before he went to be with the Lord, I talked to him about the prophetic word over his life. Both of us knew that if he wanted to make an album he needed to do it quickly. But he told me that he no longer wanted to do it because he was afraid that due to his illness it wouldn't be perfect. If it wouldn't be completely perfect, he didn't want to make an album.

After his funeral a few people talked to me about why this particular word didn't get fulfilled. I let them know what he told me. To this day I am struck by how unfortunate this was. He wasn't willing to entertain the possibility that God could have done a miracle, even in his weakness. Even if it wasn't perfect, I believe that many would have been doubly blessed simply because he had tried. I've come to realize that not everything that happens (or doesn't) is because it's God's will. There are times when we stand in the way of things that God specifically wants to do.

In 2010 Jane Hamon, a gifted and highly respected prophetic minister from the United States, gave Dick and I the following prophetic word for the Netherlands.

And the Lord says to the nation of the Netherlands, "I am releasing a fresh glory upon the land. That anti-Christ stronghold that has been over your land has been shaken in recent days. The enemy came in and the name of Islam began to claim your nation. But I have begun to raise up those with a voice of righteous indignation in your land, even those that were not believers in My name. I stirred up a holy righteous indignation in your land that is beginning to open up the heavens over the Netherlands as never before."

And the Lord says, "I want you to know that there was a time that the Netherlands missed its day of visitation. I sent a visitation upon the land not once, not twice, not three times, but I have sent My visitation five different times and the nation rejected My visitation. Yet there is a remnant in the land that has been crying out. I am hearing the voice of the remnant. My heavens are being moved by the voice of the remnant. I am removing the curse of Ichabod from your land, for the enemy has declared that the glory has departed. Instead of shame I will give double honor and double glory," says the Spirit of the Mighty God. Father, I loose that anointing now in Jesus' name.

When Dick and I heard the word we were cut to the heart and we wondered if it could be true. Could it really be that God had already tried several times to visit our nation and to pour out His Spirit and that we had rejected Him? The first part of the word about God raising up those with a voice of "righteous indignation" caught our attention. Back then there were some people, especially politicians, who were starting to be become quite vocal about the role of political Islam in the Netherlands. Often when God wants to get our attention, He will allow a prophetic word to be preceded by a word of knowledge so that we know that it's God talking. A word of knowledge is a prophetic word that gives details about a specific situation in the life of the person being prophesied over that the one prophesying could not know on their own.

After she finished prophesying, we asked Jane if she was aware of what was happening in "Holland" as she called it. She looked at us and said, "No." We told her about the political climate in the land, and this encouraged her. She then went on to tell us that during one of her earlier visits to the Netherlands, a lady had told her a story about the Netherlands and the revival in Wales back at the beginning of the twentieth century. This lady told her that her grandfather was a respected church leader in the Netherlands at the time of the Welsh revival. He and many others heard about what was happening in Wales.

Eventually it was decided that he and five other leaders of the church in the Netherlands would go to Wales to check things out to see if this was really from God. These men went and spent several weeks in Wales attending the revival services and talking to people who were involved and who were leading it. They even received prayer from the leaders of this revival with the laying on of hands.

On the way home on the boat they got together and talked. According to this lady, her grandfather and the others all agreed that what they had seen and heard was from God. Five of the six also agreed that even though this was God, it would upset too many people in their churches to have the manifestations that they had seen in Wales. Only one of them thought that it was worth the risk so that God could move. They took a vote and he lost. As a result, the revival that affected Wales and so many other places passed the Netherlands by. The lady went on to tell Jane that the man who wanted to see this move of God come to the churches eventually went to Indonesia. Revival broke out there and 1 million people came to Christ. When I think about what we missed for the sake of avoiding dissension, the only word I can think of is "tragic."

Dick and I, together with others, have been able to identify other times in our national history where people have said "no" to the move of God's Spirit. Praise the Lord that several of the current generation of leaders are now seeking to correct this by repenting of what happened back then, and God is starting to pour out His Spirit on both the Netherlands and on Europe. However, this example does demonstrate how some of the things that God wants to do can be thwarted simply because we say "no."

God spoke to me once during a time of prayer and fasting and said, "Arleen, do you know that you and Dick were not the first, second or even third couple that I called to start a church like Embassy?"

Mildly surprised, I said, "No, I didn't." I then said, "Lord, how many were there before us?"

He said, "You and Dick were the eighth couple that I called to do this." He then proceeded to show me the faces of the people he'd called before us. Their clothing changed according to the era in which they lived. It went all the way back to the revival in Wales at the beginning of the twentieth century! My heart broke and I wept as I thought about all of the people who had lived and died without knowing God during those years.

Finally, when I could talk, I asked, "Lord, why didn't they do it?"

He said, "Because they were afraid of what others would think of them if they dared to be different and start a church like this one." That was the moment I invited God to come and to weed out every ounce of the fear of man that was in my heart. Since then I've had to do even more things that have required courage. If this fear of man had remained in my heart I probably wouldn't have done them.

As prophetic people working together with apostles, we have to allow God to eliminate the fear of man from our lives. Otherwise there will come a day when God asks us to do something and we will refuse to do it because we're afraid of what others will think of us.

I go back to Genesis 1:26–28. When God gave Adam and Eve the command to "fill the earth and govern it," He delegated some of His authority to them to develop the earth on His behalf. He could have chosen to do it Himself. Instead, God chose to work together with them. Although Adam and Eve gave away this authority in Genesis 3, Jesus' death and resurrection was a major turning point. Now Jesus Himself commands us to go and disciple nations in His name. The bottom line is: our choices and our actions matter.

Called to the Marketplace

Just like the prophetic, the apostolic anointing is visionary and apostles propel people into their destiny by giving them practical steps to follow to get where they're supposed to be.

Earlier in this book I talked about our previous pastor, who had to leave the ministry after a fall. What I also need to say is that there were good times too. He was an apostle; under his ministry we learned about what it means to be apostolic.

One day this man came to Dick and said, "Why don't you think about starting your own business?" He had seen Dick's passion for ministry but knew that Dick also had a calling for the marketplace. Apostles are able to function in the other four gifts in Ephesians 4, and this man was very prophetic.

It was a simple suggestion, but Dick had never considered it before. Having his own business would mean that he'd be able to be more flexible with how he used his time. We prayed about the idea and God confirmed it to both of us pretty quickly. God also did a few miracles. One of them was that when Dick started JiL (Jesus is Lord) Consult he was able to make a flying start because he was allowed to take some of the clients he'd worked with for his former employers with him. He was also able to distinguish himself in his field, and these days they call him "The Guru" because God gives him supernatural wisdom every day to solve the problems he's confronted with. We openly give God the glory for this and are very thankful that since starting his business he has never been out of work, even for a day. In addition to this, we both get to function in ministry and to bless others financially in a way that we could never have expected before!

Healing Nations through Business

Just like we need Schools of the Prophets, we also need schools that teach us how to function in an apostolic environment. Prophecy helps us to know God's directional calling for our lives, but the apostolic helps us to get there. Within our training foundation, Living in Your Destiny, we have such a school. We call it the Kingdom Training School, and through it we've seen people become much clearer about what they're called to do and how they're called to walk it out.

Three years ago we had a married couple in one of our schools who were searching for God's will for their lives. The husband was an executive at a large international company and he was on the fast-track to becoming a vice president in one of their divisions. The only problem was that he wasn't happy. He is an extremely gifted photographer and thought that maybe he was called to go into photography. An important element of our Kingdom Training Schools is that we help people discover which of the seven mountains they are called to. We teach them how to ask God for a revelation of what He wants them to do. They learn how to make a business plan to finance it. I speak to each of the students individually about this and I prophesy over them. To this couple's surprise, and mine, I heard myself prophesying to this couple about God calling them to start their own business. This wasn't anywhere on their radar.

A few months later, they contacted me and told me that God had spoken to them Himself about the fact that He wanted them to start their own business. The big question, however, was: "What kind of business and how?" Just when they had decided they would start a business, the company he worked for asked him to head up a project to open a major new office of theirs in southern India. This threw them for a loop. At this stage they came back to me and asked if God had let me see where He wanted them to be. I looked up at them and said, "When God spoke to me about your starting your own business I saw people who looked like they were from Africa." That helped them because they had seen that too.

From then on they started reading and consciously asking God daily to lead them. About a year later they started their own company "Lydia Trade." Their aim—to help lift African entrepreneurs out of poverty by connecting them to the global market. Since then they've also started several other companies and are increasingly active on the African continent. Even though they've had their challenges, like all starting entrepreneurs, they are fulfilled and really enjoy what they're doing. They tell me now: "We were made for this!"

Promotion

Another lady, Esther, worked in a daycare center, in what was in effect a dead-end job. She also signed up for the Kingdom Training School. She was a gifted organizer but had no outlet for her talents where she worked. The only good thing about her job was that she loved working with children. She knew, however, that she was created for more.

During her deployment phase, she and I had a talk. In addition to being a prophet I am also a DISC Personality Analysis trainer. Years ago I noticed that while prophecy helped me to see what people were called to do, DISC allowed me to help them to better understand how they communicate and in what kind of settings they function best. So a DISC-analysis is part of the school's program.

During our meeting I asked the Lord for a prophetic word for her. He showed me that He was going to open the door for promotion at her work. I also prophesied that God had given her leadership gifts and that she would use them at her work. She laughed when she heard this because in her situation that would never happen (or so she thought). I also discussed her DISC results with her. I hadn't looked at them before going into the meeting. Not only did the results show that she was a leader, but that she would thrive in a position of leadership.

Two months later, her department head needed to travel for work for a few weeks and asked Esther if she would take the lead while the head was gone. She agreed to do it and did it well. When her department head returned, she told Esther that she was being promoted to have regional oversight of the network of child daycare centers. She also told Esther that even though Esther didn't have the official qualifications, she had recommended that she be promoted to department head of that particular location. I saw Esther a few days after this had happened and she told me that it was the prophetic word together with the DISC results that gave her the courage to say yes.

I could tell many more stories about how God has used the prophetic working together with the apostolic to transform lives, but that is for another book. I hope that I've shown you with this book how you can come to action in your sphere. Listen to God's voice, test what you've heard and then work together to act on what He's shown you. In that way you will learn how to work together with Him through revelation. It is the best way to see God's Kingdom advanced on the earth. This is how you prophecy and change the world. This is how you have impact!

Prophetic Code of Conduct

1. God's character in me is more important than my gifts. My prophesying will always exalt Jesus Christ and bring people closer to the Father.
2. I commit myself to living a life free from uncleanness, addictions, bitterness and the love of success in the eyes of people.
3. I will, through my prophesying, encourage, comfort and build up the body of Christ so that it becomes more and more like Christ and hungry for God.
4. I will not ask for payment for a prophetic word and I will not give people the idea that the revelation I receive can be influenced by a gift.
5. I will prophesy truth with mercy and without condemning the one for whom the word is meant. Hope for change through the power of Jesus Christ will be at the center of my message.
6. I strive to be accurate in the prophetic and use the Bible as the undisputed standard for evaluating every revelation.
7. I will not bring separation in the body of Christ and will not use my prophetic gifting carelessly.
8. I will not prophesy in a way that controls or manipulates others and I will always encourage those I prophesy over to test my prophetic words.
9. I will admit when I'm wrong and take steps to repair the damage where possible.

10. I will allow supernatural manifestations of the Holy Spirit without glorying in them or allowing them to distract the attention from the Lord.
11. I will honor the leaders who God has appointed. I will encourage them and discuss with them the revelation that I receive.
12. I will not be arrogant. I will fear God and I will not fear man or the loss of popularity or opportunities if I prophesy what God wants me to say.
13. I dedicate myself to prayer and worship. I commit myself to studying the Bible and the ways of God.
14. I act with integrity. I treat information as confidential and will not misuse the knowledge that God shares with me through revelation.
15. I seek out mature, trustworthy people to be accountable to and to help me to grow in prophetic ministry. I will share and discuss this code of conduct with them.

This prophetic code of conduct was developed by the Netherlands Prophetic Council in collaboration with Living in Your Destiny.[24] A more detailed treatment of this whole area of protocol can be found in the article "Biblical Principles Concerning Ethics and Protocols Related to New Testament Prophetic Ministry" by Marc Dupont and John Paul Jackson.[25]

Recommended Reading

DELIVERANCE, INNER HEALING AND FREEDOM FROM GENERATIONAL CURSES

Anderson, N. T., *The Bondage Breaker. Overcoming Negative Thoughts, Irrational Feelings, Habitual Sins* (Eugene, OR: Harvest House Publishers, 1997).

Anderson, N.T., Vander Hook, P., Vander Hook, S., *Spiritual Protection for Your Children: Helping Your Children and Family Find Their Identity, Freedom and Security in Christ* (Raleigh, NC: Regal House Publishing, 1996).

Kylstra, C. & Kylstra, B., *Restoring the Foundations: The Integrated Approach To Healing Ministry* (Mount Juliet, TN: Proclaiming His Word Publications, 2007).

Murphy, E., *The Handbook for Spiritual Warfare* (Nashville, TN: Thomas Nelson Publishers, 1996).

Prince, D., *They Shall Expel Demons: What You Need to Know About Demons, Your Invisible Enemies* (Grand Rapids, MI: Baker Publishing Group, 1998).

Prince, D., *Blessing or Curse: You Can Choose* (Grand Rapids, MI: Chosen Books, 1990).

Van, M.T., *Acquittal. How to Pray for Deliverance for Yourself from the Courts of Heaven* (Amsterdam: Mandate Publishing, 2019).

DELIVERANCE MINISTRIES IN THE NETHERLANDS

Living in Your Destiny: liyd.org

Vrij Zijn: vrijzijn.nl

PROPHECY

Bolz, S., *Translating God: Hearing God's Voice for Yourself and the World Around You* (Glendale, CA: Newtype Publishing, 2015).

Bolz, S., *God Secrets* (Glendale, CA: Newtype Publishing, 2017).

Campbell, S., Campbell W., *Ecstatic Prophecy* (Grand Rapids, MI: Chosen Books, 2008).

Cooke, G., *Prophecy and Responsibility: A Journey into Receiving Revelation and the Process of Godly Communication* (Vancouver, BC: Brilliant Book House, 2007).

Cooke, G., *Approaching the Heart of Prophecy: A Journey into Encouragement, Blessings and Prophetic Gifting* (Vancouver, BC: Brilliant Book House, 2009).

Cooke, G. *Prophetic Wisdom* (Vancouver, BC: Brilliant Book House, 2010).

Goll, J., *The Seer: The Prophetic Power of Visions, Dreams, and Open Heavens* (Shippensburg, PA: Destiny Image, 2004).

Goll, J., *The Lifestyle of a Prophet* (Grand Rapids, MI: Chosen Books, 2013).

Goll, J., *The Discerner: Hearing, Confirming, Acting on Prophetic Revelation* (New Kensington, PA: Whitaker House, 2017).

Hamon, J., *Dreams and Visions* (Raleigh, NC: Regal House Publishing, 2000).

Helland, M., *Prophesy—Just Do It!* (North Palm Beach, FL: Arrowz USA, 2019).

Jacobs, C., *The Voice of God* (Raleigh, NC: Regal House Publishing, 1995).

Jacobs, C., *The Reformation Manifesto: Your Part in God's Plan to Change Nations Today* (Bloomington, MN: Bethany House, 2008).

Vallotton, K., *Basic Training for the Prophetic Ministry* (Shippensburg, PA: Destiny Image, 2014).

Vallotton, K., *School of the Prophets: Advanced Training for Prophetic Ministry.* (Grand Rapids, MI: Chosen Books, 2015).

REFORMATION, TRANSFORMATION AND THE 7 MOUNTAIN MANDATE

Ahn, C., *Modern-Day Apostles: Operating in Your Apostolic Office and Anointing* (Shippensburg, PA: Destiny Image, 2019).

Caron, A., *Apostolic Centers: Shifting the Church, Transforming the World* (Vancouver, BC: Arsenal Pulp Press, 2013).

Cuny, P. L., *Nehemiah People: Destiny and Purpose Rediscovered Through the Nehemiah Template* (Clifton, NJ: Doxa Publishing, 2014).

Eberle, H.R., *The Complete Wineskin* (Yakima, WA: Worldcast Publishing, 1993).

Eberle, H.R., Garfield, J., *Releasing Kings for Ministry in the Marketplace* (Yakima, WA: Worldcast Publishing, 2014).

Enlow, J., *The Seven Mountain Prophecy: Unveiling the Coming Elijah Revolution* (Lake Mary, FL: Creation House, 2008).

Enlow, J., *The Seven Mountain Mantle: Receiving the Joseph Anointing to Reform Nations* (New Kensington, PA: Whitaker House, 2017).

Enlow, J., *The Seven Mountain Renaissance: Vision and Strategy Through 2050* (New Kensington, PA: Whitaker House, 2015).

Femrite, T., *Invading the Seven Mountains with Intercession: How to Reclaim Society Through Prayer.* (New Kensington, PA: Whitaker House, 2011).

Hague, W., *William Wilberforce: The Life of the Great Anti-Slave Trade Campaigner* (London: Harper Perennial, 2008).

Hamon, B., *Apostles, Prophets and the Coming Moves of God: God's End-Time Plans for His Church and Planet Earth* (Shippensburg, PA: Destiny Image, 1997).

Hillman, O., *Change Agent: Engaging Your Passion to be the One Who Makes a Difference* (Lake Mary, FL: Creation House, 2011).

Lyons, G., *The Next Christians: Seven Ways You Can Live the Gospel and Restore the World* (New York: The Crown Publishing Group, 2010).

Mattera, J., *Ruling in the Gates: Preparing the Church to Transform Cities* (Lake Mary, FL: Creation House, 2003).

Mattera, J., *Understanding the Wineskin of the Kingdom* (Chambersburg, PA: eGenCo., 2016)

Silvoso, E., *Transformation: Change the Marketplace and You Change the World* (Raleigh, NC: Regal House Publishing, 2007).

Silvoso, E., *Ekklesia: Rediscovering God's Instrument for Global Transformation* (Grand Rapids, MI: Chosen Books, 2014).

Vallotton, K., *Heavy Rain: How to Flood Your World with God's Transforming Power* (Grand Rapids, MI: Chosen Books, 2016).

Wagner, C.P., *Apostles Today: Biblical Government for Biblical Power* (Raleigh, NC: Regal House Publishing, 2006).

Wagner, C.P., *Dominion! How Kingdom Action Can Change the World* (Grand Rapids, MI: Chosen Books, 2008).

Wagner, C.P., *This Changes Everything: How God Can Transform Your Mind and Change Your Life* (Raleigh, NC: Regal Books, 2013).

Notes

INTRODUCTION

1. Mammon is an idol. The word "Mammon" is Aramaic for "money" or "riches" and refers to money being worshiped as a god. It is generally acknowledged to be the spiritual root behind greed and Jesus said in Matthew 6:24 "you cannot serve God and Mammon."
2. britannica.com/biography/James-Watt, accessed May 23, 2019.
3. Based on Klaus Schwab, *The Fourth Industrial Revolution* (London: Portfolio Penguin, 2016), p. 3.
4. Ibid., p. 38.
5. The word "apostle" means "sent one." Apostles were those sent out by the Roman government of Jesus' time with the assignment to change the culture of the newly conquered territories so that they became more like Rome. Jesus called his twelve disciples apostles after He gave them authority and sent them out to demonstrate God's Kingdom rule on the earth. (Luke 9:2). Their mandate was to make the earth look more like heaven. Our mandate is the same as theirs—to make the earth look more like heaven and to demonstrate God's Kingdom rule in every nation and sphere of influence on the planet.
6. The "Seven Mountains" are seven spheres of influence in society that influence and mold the way we think. Our cultures are shaped by these spheres (mountains) and society is changed and transformed through all seven: economy, family, education, religion/spirituality, media, celebration and government (www.the7mountains.com, accessed May 23, 2019). The "Seven Mountains" are a reference to Revelation 17:9.

CHAPTER 1

7. Dr. Paul Kennedy, *NRC Handelsblad*, October 29, 2011.
8. elijahlist.com/words/display_word.html?ID=10524, accessed May 9, 2019.
9. The Marketplace Movement refers to the fact that God wants to use the 97–98 percent of Christians who are not in traditional "full-time" church ministry to advance His Kingdom here on the earth. He does this by using us to bring transformation in people's lives, our workplaces and our societies through the power of his Holy Spirit.
10. *The Brewery Journal*, "Exploring Mutuality" (London: The Brewery Ltd., 2014), p. 3.

CHAPTER 3

11. An "apostolic center" is a group of ministries and organizations that are started by an apostle, that includes a church, and that is releasing believers to have impact in every single sphere of influence in society. It is different from an "apostolic church" that is a church, started by an apostle, which is releasing people into ministry in the church sphere.
12. Inspired by James W. Goll, *The Lifestyle Of A Prophet* (Ada, MI: Chosen Books, 2001) p. 106 – 107.

CHAPTER 4

13. Jane Hamon, *Dreams and Visions* (Ventura, CA: Regal Books, 1997), p. 55.
14. Ibid., p. 17.

CHAPTER 7

15. For more information, see 'Recommended Reading'.

CHAPTER 8

16. I am indebted to the excellent blog, fireschoolministries.com/blog/2016/1/25/breaking-an-orphan-mindset for this list (accessed February 19, 2019.)

CHAPTER 9

17. Prophetic pioneer Dr. Bill Hamon has written an excellent book about this: *How Can These Things Be?* (Shippensburg, PA: Destiny Image, 2015).
18. Author unknown, quoted in J. Oswald Sanders, *Spiritual Leadership* (Chicago, IL: Moody Press, 1967), p. 141.

CHAPTER 10

19. James D. Bratt, *Abraham Kuyper: Modern Calvinist, Christian Democrat* (Grand Rapids, MI: William B. Eerdmans Publishing Company, 2013), p. 195.

CHAPTER 11

20. elijahlist.com/words/display_word.html?ID=10524, accessed May 9, 2019.
21. en.wikipedia.org/wiki/List_of_Jewish_Nobel_laureates, accessed May 9, 2019.
22. jbuff.com/c010407.htm, accessed May 9, 2019.

CHAPTER 12

23. In the NKJV.

APPENDIX

24. © 2014 Stichting Living in Your Destiny / The Netherlands Prophetic Council.
25. marcdupontministries.com/biblical-principles-ethics-protocols-new-testament-prophetic-ministry, accessed May 9, 2019.

arleenwesterhof.com
facebook.com/arleenwesterhof

About the Author

Arleen Westerhof is the Lead Pastor of the God's Embassy Church in Amsterdam, the Netherlands, together with her husband Dick. Founded in 2005, God's Embassy is a cutting-edge apostolic center with an anointing for reformation and transformation. Through obedience to the voice of God they have seen measurable positive change occur in the Red Light District near to them.

Arleen is an international conference speaker and the founder and director of the Netherlands Prophetic Council and of the Living In Your Destiny Schools of the Prophets. These schools, which are highly esteemed among both church and marketplace leaders, provide comprehensive training in the prophetic. Graduates can be found operating in their prophetic gifting both in their churches and in their spheres of influence in society. She is also the founder of the Economic Summit that exists to provide divinely inspired solutions for global economic problems. Since its inception in 2014, it has become an internationally respected organization that advises governments and businesses on strategies for national transformation.

As an international speaker, Arleen trains people from all walks of life to discern the voice of God for their own lives, ministries, businesses and cities. Arleen has a Ph.D. in chemistry from the University of Western Ontario in Canada and completed a Postdoctoral Research Fellowship at the University of London (England) before being recruited to work for a large multinational company in Amsterdam. Her experience in the business world, ministry, consultancy and education all combine to give her unique insights into how to effect change.

She is a gifted communicator and her prophetic insight and balanced teaching have led to her to becoming a respected voice on the prophetic and an advisor to leaders worldwide.

Dick and Arleen live in Amsterdam.

Promised

—A Creative Journey from Head to Heart

Allow God's promises to land in your heart

The Bible is a storehouse full of promises about who God is for us. He says, "I am powerful. Just trust Me!" God desires to have an intimate relationship with us. With each promise that He makes, He seeks to draw us closer to Himself. Dare we trust Him, even in our struggles?

Promised shares 21 key promises from the Bible. Each of these promises is accompanied by a creative assignment to help it land in our hearts. We'll color, write, and learn how to do Bible journaling and hand lettering. We'll contemplate God's promises, sing, and pray about them. We will learn to stand on God's promises, and live with a song in our hearts.

Suitable for both individual and group use.

SADDLE STITCH
48 PAGES
8.5 x 0.2 x 11.0 in
ISBN 9781951014001
RRP $12.99

CAROLYN ROS has worked as a teacher, tutor, and coach for Youth with a Mission in Amsterdam, the Netherlands. She and her husband have four adult children and nine grandchildren. In her turbulent life, Carolyn has experienced that God does what He has promised.

PROPHESY *JUST DO IT!*

You Can Prophesy

Would you be willing to prophesy if it were God's will for you to do so? It is His will! The Bible says, "You can all prophesy one by one, so that all may learn and all be encouraged" (1 Cor. 14:31).

Discover how you can nurture and develop your ability to hear God's voice and prophesy. With more than thirty practical exercises, you can learn (individually or in a group) how to distinguish God's voice and how to prophesy well. Be encouraged by the testimonies and anecdotes that demonstrate the power of prophecy. Don't hold back. *Prophesy—Just Do It!*

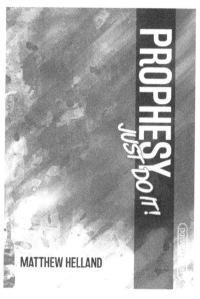

MATTHEW HELLAND

POWERPOCKET
144 PAGES
4.7 X 0.4 X 6.7 IN
ISBN 9789490489526
RRP $12.99

MATTHEW HELLAND (M.Div., Oral Roberts University) has led schools of prophecy around the world since 2010. Together with his wife, Femke, he works as a pastor in Amsterdam's Red-Light District. Matt and Femke have four children.

ARROWZ

Cutting-Edge Materials
for Radical Followers of Jesus

Visit us at
arrowz.org

For questions and bulk discount orders
please contact us at info@arrowz.org

Lightning Source UK Ltd.
Milton Keynes UK
UKHW010630121121
393852UK00001B/89